HOW CENTRAL BANK DIGITAL CURRENCIES WILL
RESHAPE THE GLOBAL FINANCIAL SYSTEM

THE FUTURE
OF MONEY

JOSH LUBERISSE

THE FUTURE
OF MONEY

How Central Bank Digital Currencies Will Reshape The Global Financial System

Josh Luberisse

Fortis Novum Mundum

CONTENTS

TABLE OF CONTENTS

PREFACE

The dawn of the digital age has ushered in a transformative era for the global financial system. The rapid advancement of technology has revolutionized traditional banking, investments, and currency transactions, paving the way for new and innovative financial instruments. Among these innovations, Central Bank Digital Currencies (CBDCs) stand out as a profound development that promises to reshape the very foundation of monetary systems worldwide.

In the early 21st century, the rise of cryptocurrencies like Bitcoin and Ethereum sparked a financial revolution. These decentralized digital currencies challenged the hegemony of traditional fiat currencies and introduced the concept of a borderless, decentralized financial system. However, alongside the opportunities came significant challenges, including volatility, regulatory uncertainty, and questions about scalability and security. It was against this backdrop that central banks around the world began to explore the potential of issuing their own digital currencies.

CBDCs represent a hybrid approach, combining the stability and trust associated with central banks with the technological advancements of blockchain and distributed ledger technologies. Unlike cryptocurrencies, CBDCs are issued and regulated by central banks, ensuring a level of oversight and stability that is absent in the largely unregulated cryptocurrency markets. This unique positioning allows CBDCs to offer the benefits of digital currencies—such as faster transactions and lower costs—while maintaining the integrity and security of traditional financial systems.

The introduction of CBDCs is not merely a technological upgrade but a fundamental shift in the way we conceive of money and monetary policy. Central banks, the custodians of monetary stability, are now at the forefront of this digital transformation. Their foray into digital currencies is driven by a multitude of factors, including the need to enhance financial inclusion, improve payment efficiency, and counter the growing influence of private cryptocurrencies.

In exploring the impact of CBDCs on the global financial system, this book delves into the multifaceted implications of this innovation. From the transformation of international trade and investment flows to the redefinition of monetary policy and financial stability, the advent of CBDCs heralds a new era of financial architecture. The potential of CBDCs to enhance cross-border payments, reduce transaction costs, and foster economic inclusivity is immense. However, their implementation also poses significant challenges, including regulatory harmonization, technological integration, and the safeguarding of privacy and security.

The journey of understanding CBDCs involves navigating complex terrains of technology, economics, and policy. This book aims to provide a comprehensive and authoritative examination of these themes, offering insights into how CBDCs can be effectively integrated into the existing financial framework while addressing the challenges that accompany their adoption. It brings together perspectives from leading experts in finance, technology, and policy-making to present a holistic view of the future of money in the digital age.

As we stand on the brink of a new financial frontier, it is imperative to understand the dynamics of CBDCs and their far-reaching implications. This book is an invitation to explore the potential of digital currencies to transform the global financial system, offering a roadmap for navigating the complexities and opportunities of this exciting new landscape. Through rigorous analysis and thoughtful discourse, we aim to illuminate the path forward, guiding policymakers, financial professionals, and global citizens toward a future where money is not just a medium of exchange but a catalyst for innovation and inclusivity.

INTRODUCTION

Global Significance of Central Bank Digital Currencies (CBDCs)

The concept of money has undergone profound transformations throughout human history, from barter systems to the adoption of coins, paper currency, and digital payments. Each shift has brought about fundamental changes in the way economies operate, influencing trade, commerce, and societal development. Today, we stand at the cusp of another revolutionary change with the advent of Central Bank Digital Currencies (CBDCs). This introduction aims to provide a comprehensive understanding of CBDCs, exploring their origins, the motivations behind their development, and their potential impact on the global financial system.

Central Bank Digital Currencies represent a new form of digital money issued directly by central banks. Unlike traditional fiat currencies, which exist in physical form as banknotes and coins, or as digital records in commercial bank accounts, CBDCs are entirely digital and are a direct liability of the central bank. This distinction is crucial as it places CBDCs at the heart of the monetary system, offering a level of security and trust that private cryptocurrencies and other digital assets cannot match.

The genesis of CBDCs can be traced back to the increasing digitalization of economies and the rise of cryptocurrencies. The introduction of Bitcoin in 2009 by an anonymous entity known as Satoshi Nakamoto marked the beginning of a new era in digital finance. Bitcoin and subsequent cryptocurrencies introduced the idea of decentralized, peer-to-peer transactions without the need for intermediaries. This innovation was based on blockchain technology, a decentralized ledger system that ensures transparency and security.

While cryptocurrencies garnered significant attention and investment, they also presented challenges such as high volatility, regulatory uncertainties, and concerns over their use in illicit activities. Central banks recognized the need to harness the benefits of digital currencies while mitigating these risks. Thus, the concept of CBDCs was born. By leveraging the underlying technology of cryptocurrencies, central banks sought to create a digital currency that could serve as a stable and secure medium of exchange, store of value, and unit of account.

The motivations for developing CBDCs are manifold. One of the primary drivers is the desire to enhance payment efficiency. Traditional payment systems, especially for cross-border transactions, are often slow, expensive, and opaque. CBDCs have the potential to streamline these processes, reducing transaction costs and settlement times while increasing transparency. This efficiency can significantly benefit businesses and consumers, fostering greater economic activity and integration.

Financial inclusion is another critical motivation behind CBDCs. Despite advancements in financial technology, a significant portion of the global population remains unbanked or underbanked. CBDCs can provide a more accessible and inclusive financial system by offering digital payment solutions that do not require a traditional bank account. This can empower individuals in remote or underserved regions, enabling them to participate in the formal economy and access financial services.

Moreover, CBDCs can enhance monetary policy effectiveness.

Central banks use various tools to influence economic activity and maintain price stability, such as interest rates and reserve requirements. However, these tools can be blunt and indirect. With CBDCs, central banks can have a more direct impact on money supply and demand. For instance, they could implement programmable money with specific attributes, such as expiration dates or spending limits, to encourage or discourage certain economic behaviors.

The global significance of CBDCs extends beyond national borders. In an interconnected world, the introduction of CBDCs by major economies can have ripple effects across the global financial system. For example, the adoption of a digital yuan by China has sparked discussions about the potential for CBDCs to shift the balance of economic power and influence international trade dynamics. Similarly, the European Central Bank's exploration of a digital euro reflects the growing recognition of CBDCs' strategic importance in maintaining monetary sovereignty and competitiveness.

However, the implementation of CBDCs is not without challenges. One of the foremost concerns is the impact on financial stability. The introduction of CBDCs could disrupt traditional banking models, as individuals and businesses might prefer holding digital currency directly with the central bank rather than in commercial bank accounts. This could lead to disintermediation, where banks lose their role as intermediaries in the financial system, potentially reducing their capacity to lend and manage liquidity.

Privacy and security are also critical considerations. While CBDCs can offer greater transparency in transactions, this transparency must be balanced with the need to protect individual privacy. Ensuring robust cybersecurity measures to safeguard against digital threats is paramount to maintaining trust in the new system. Additionally, regulatory frameworks must evolve to address the unique characteristics of digital currencies, ensuring that they are integrated into the broader financial system without creating regulatory arbitrage or loopholes.

As we explore the landscape of CBDCs, it is essential to consider the diverse approaches taken by different countries. Each nation's economic, political, and social context shapes its strategy for developing and implementing a digital currency. For instance, China's digital yuan project is part of a broader effort to increase digital infrastructure and reduce reliance on the traditional banking system. In contrast, the European Central Bank's digital euro initiative emphasizes maintaining monetary sovereignty and enhancing payment efficiency within the eurozone.

In the following chapters, we will delve deeper into these themes, examining the technological foundations of CBDCs, the various design choices and trade-offs, and the potential implications for monetary policy, financial stability, and global trade. Through a rigorous analysis of current developments and future trends, we aim to provide a comprehensive understanding of how Central Bank Digital Currencies will reshape the global financial system. This journey will illuminate the path forward, highlighting the opportunities and challenges that lie ahead as we transition into a new era of digital money.

CHAPTER 1: THE NEW FINANCIAL ECOSYSTEM

1.1 Transformation of Financial Landscapes through Digital Technologies

The financial ecosystem has undergone a profound transformation driven by the rapid advancements in digital technologies. These changes have redefined the ways in which financial services are delivered, accessed, and utilized, ushering in an era characterized by enhanced efficiency, inclusivity, and innovation. To understand the impact of Central Bank Digital Currencies (CBDCs) within this context, it is essential to explore how digital technologies have reshaped the financial landscape.

The genesis of this transformation can be traced back to the early adoption of digital payment systems and online banking. Initially, these innovations provided convenience and accessibility, allowing consumers to perform transactions without visiting physical bank branches. Over time, the proliferation of smartphones and internet connectivity further accelerated this shift, making digital financial services ubiquitous.

One of the most significant developments in this digital

revolution has been the advent of blockchain technology. Introduced in 2009 with the creation of Bitcoin, blockchain is a decentralized ledger system that enables secure, transparent, and tamper-proof transactions. This technology challenged traditional financial paradigms by eliminating the need for intermediaries, such as banks, in verifying and processing transactions. The decentralized nature of blockchain promised a more democratized and resilient financial system, where trust is established through cryptographic algorithms rather than centralized institutions.

Blockchain technology's most notable application has been in the realm of cryptocurrencies. Cryptocurrencies like Bitcoin, Ethereum, and others have gained substantial traction, both as speculative investments and as alternative means of payment. Their decentralized and borderless nature has made them appealing to those seeking to bypass traditional banking systems, whether for ideological reasons, efficiency, or in regions with unstable financial systems.

The rise of cryptocurrencies has not only introduced new financial instruments but also catalyzed the development of decentralized finance (DeFi). DeFi platforms leverage blockchain technology to recreate traditional financial services, such as lending, borrowing, and trading, in a decentralized manner. These platforms operate without intermediaries, relying instead on smart contracts—self-executing contracts with the terms of the agreement directly written into code. DeFi represents a significant leap in financial innovation, offering more accessible and efficient financial services, particularly in regions where traditional banking infrastructure is lacking.

While blockchain and cryptocurrencies have garnered significant attention, the broader impact of digital technologies on finance extends beyond these innovations. The financial technology (fintech) sector has emerged as a powerhouse of creativity and disruption, introducing new business models and solutions across the financial spectrum. Fintech companies have revolutionized areas such as payments, lending, insurance, and wealth management by leveraging technologies like artificial intelligence (AI), machine learning, and big data analytics.

In the payments space, fintech innovations have led to the development of digital wallets and mobile payment systems. Companies like PayPal, Square, and Alipay have transformed how consumers and businesses conduct transactions, offering seamless and instantaneous payment solutions. These digital wallets have also played a crucial role in promoting financial inclusion by providing banking services to the unbanked and underbanked populations.

Lending has similarly been transformed by digital technologies. Online lending platforms use AI and machine learning algorithms to assess creditworthiness and provide loans with greater speed and accuracy than traditional banks. This has expanded access to credit for individuals and small businesses, particularly those who may not meet the stringent criteria of conventional lenders.

In the insurance industry, insurtech startups are leveraging digital tools to streamline processes, enhance customer experiences, and offer personalized products. By using data analytics and AI, these companies can better assess risks, reduce fraud, and tailor insurance policies to individual needs. This has led to more efficient and customer-centric insurance services.

Wealth management has also benefited from the digital revolution. Robo-advisors, which use algorithms to provide investment advice and portfolio management, have democratized access to financial planning. These platforms offer low-cost, automated investment solutions, making wealth management accessible to a broader audience.

The integration of big data analytics has further revolutionized financial services. Financial institutions now have access to vast amounts of data that can be analyzed to gain insights into customer behavior, market trends, and risk factors. This data-driven approach enables more informed decision-making, personalized customer experiences, and proactive risk management.

As digital technologies continue to evolve, they are increasingly intersecting with emerging trends such as the Internet of Things (IoT) and 5G connectivity. The IoT, which connects everyday objects to the internet, has the potential to transform various aspects of finance, from enabling real-time transaction monitoring to enhancing supply chain financing. Similarly, 5G connectivity promises to accelerate the adoption of digital financial services by providing faster and more reliable internet connections, particularly in remote and underserved areas.

Amidst these technological advancements, central banks and financial regulators are grappling with the need to adapt and ensure the stability and integrity of the financial system. The rise of digital currencies and decentralized finance presents both opportunities and challenges. On one hand, these innovations can enhance financial inclusion, reduce transaction costs, and increase transparency. On the other hand, they pose risks related to security, privacy, and financial stability.

Central banks have recognized the transformative potential of digital technologies and are actively exploring the development of CBDCs. Unlike cryptocurrencies, which operate outside the purview of central authorities, CBDCs are digital representations of a country's fiat currency issued and regulated by the central bank. This unique characteristic positions CBDCs to offer the benefits of digital currencies while maintaining the stability and oversight associated with traditional monetary systems.

The introduction of CBDCs is expected to further accelerate the transformation of the financial landscape. By providing a secure and efficient medium of exchange, CBDCs can facilitate faster and cheaper transactions, both domestically and internationally. They can also enhance the effectiveness of monetary policy by providing central banks with real-time data on money supply and demand. Moreover, CBDCs have the potential to foster greater financial inclusion by offering digital payment solutions that are accessible to all segments of society.

The transformation of the financial landscape through digital technologies has been nothing short of revolutionary. From the rise of cryptocurrencies and DeFi to the proliferation of fintech innovations, these advancements have reshaped how financial services are delivered and consumed. Central Bank Digital Currencies represent the next frontier in this digital revolution, promising to redefine the future of money and finance. As we navigate this evolving landscape, it is essential to understand the opportunities and challenges presented by these technologies and to develop strategies that harness their potential for the benefit of all.

1.2 Rise of Fintech: Evolution and Impact

The rise of financial technology, commonly known as fintech, has been one of the most transformative developments in the financial sector over the past few decades. Fintech refers to the integration of technology into offerings by financial services companies to improve their use and delivery to consumers. This movement has fundamentally altered the landscape of finance, affecting everything from payments and lending to insurance and wealth management.

The evolution of fintech can be traced back to the late 20th century when financial institutions began to adopt early forms of digital technology. Automated Teller Machines (ATMs), online banking, and electronic stock trading platforms marked the initial steps toward a more digital financial ecosystem. These innovations laid the groundwork for the fintech explosion that would follow in the early 21st century.

The advent of the internet and the proliferation of mobile devices provided the critical infrastructure necessary for fintech to thrive. The widespread availability of high-speed internet and smartphones opened new avenues for financial services delivery, enabling companies to reach consumers in ways that were previously unimaginable. Mobile banking apps, peer-to-peer payment systems, and digital wallets became mainstream, offering unprecedented convenience and accessibility.

One of the most significant milestones in the fintech revolution was the emergence of online payment systems. Companies like PayPal pioneered the concept of digital payments, allowing users to send and receive money electronically without the need for traditional banking intermediaries. This innovation not only simplified transactions but also democratized access to financial services, particularly for individuals and small businesses.

The rise of fintech was further fueled by the 2008 financial crisis, which exposed vulnerabilities in the traditional banking system and eroded public trust in established financial institutions. In the aftermath of the crisis, there was a growing demand for more transparent, efficient, and customer-centric financial services. This environment provided fertile ground for fintech startups to flourish, as they sought to address the shortcomings of the incumbent players.

Fintech's impact on the payments industry has been profound. Digital wallets and mobile payment platforms, such as Apple Pay, Google Wallet, and Alipay, have transformed the way people conduct transactions. These platforms enable users to make payments quickly and securely using their smartphones, bypassing the need for cash or physical cards. The convenience and speed of mobile payments have driven their widespread adoption, particularly among younger generations.

In addition to revolutionizing payments, fintech has had a transformative effect on the lending industry. Traditional lending processes often involve lengthy paperwork, stringent credit assessments, and significant wait times for approval. Fintech companies have streamlined this process by leveraging data analytics and machine learning to assess creditworthiness more accurately and efficiently. Online lending platforms like LendingClub and Prosper use algorithms to evaluate borrowers' financial profiles, enabling faster loan approvals and disbursements. This has expanded access to credit for individuals and small businesses who may not meet the criteria of traditional lenders.

The insurance sector, too, has been significantly impacted by fintech. Insurtech startups are harnessing digital tools to enhance the efficiency and customer experience of insurance services. These companies use big data and AI to assess risk more precisely, streamline claims processing, and offer personalized insurance products. For example, companies like Lemonade and Root Insurance have introduced innovative models that leverage technology to provide more affordable and customer-friendly insurance solutions.

Wealth management is another area where fintech has made substantial inroads. The advent of robo-advisors— automated platforms that provide investment advice based on algorithms—has democratized access to wealth management services. Platforms like Betterment and Wealthfront offer low-cost, automated investment solutions, making it easier for individuals to invest and manage their portfolios. These services use advanced algorithms to assess risk tolerance, goals, and market conditions, providing personalized investment strategies that were once only available to high-net-worth individuals through traditional financial advisors.

The integration of big data analytics has further amplified

fintech's impact. Financial institutions now have access to vast amounts of data that can be analyzed to gain insights into customer behavior, market trends, and risk factors. This data-driven approach enables more informed decision-making, personalized customer experiences, and proactive risk management. For instance, banks can use data analytics to detect fraudulent activities in real time, while insurers can leverage data to offer dynamic pricing based on individual risk profiles.

Blockchain technology, often associated with cryptocurrencies, has also played a crucial role in the fintech revolution. Beyond its use in digital currencies, blockchain offers a secure, transparent, and immutable ledger system that can be applied to various financial services. Smart contracts, which are self-executing contracts with the terms of the agreement directly written into code, have the potential to automate and streamline complex financial transactions. Blockchain's decentralized nature reduces the need for intermediaries, lowering costs and increasing transaction speed and security.

Fintech's evolution has not only transformed individual financial services but has also given rise to new business models and ecosystems. Peer-to-peer (P2P) lending platforms, crowdfunding sites, and digital challenger banks are just a few examples of the innovative models that have emerged. P2P lending platforms connect borrowers directly with lenders, bypassing traditional banks and offering more competitive interest rates. Crowdfunding sites like Kickstarter and Indiegogo enable entrepreneurs to raise funds directly from the public, democratizing access to capital. Digital challenger banks, such as N26 and Monzo, operate entirely online, offering a range of banking services without the overhead costs associated with physical branches.

The rise of fintech has also prompted traditional financial institutions to innovate and adapt. Banks and insurance companies have embraced digital transformation, investing in technology to enhance their services and remain competitive. Many have formed partnerships with fintech startups to leverage their technological expertise and innovative solutions. This collaboration between incumbents and fintech firms has led to a more dynamic and interconnected financial ecosystem.

The impact of fintech extends beyond developed markets. In emerging economies, fintech has played a pivotal role in advancing financial inclusion. Mobile money services, such as M-Pesa in Kenya, have provided millions of unbanked individuals with access to financial services, enabling them to save, borrow, and transfer money using their mobile phones. These services have not only empowered individuals but have also contributed to economic growth and development.

As fintech continues to evolve, it faces several challenges and regulatory considerations. Ensuring the security and privacy of digital transactions is paramount, as cyber threats and data breaches pose significant risks. Regulators must strike a balance between fostering innovation and protecting consumers, ensuring that fintech companies operate within a framework that maintains financial stability and integrity. Additionally, the rapid pace of technological change requires continuous adaptation and collaboration between regulators, financial institutions, and fintech firms.

The rise of fintech has revolutionized the financial landscape, introducing new technologies, business models, and services that have enhanced efficiency, accessibility, and customer experience. From payments and lending to insurance and wealth management, fintech has redefined the way financial services are delivered and consumed. As we move forward, the continued integration of digital technologies and the development of innovative solutions will shape the future of finance, creating a more inclusive, efficient, and resilient financial ecosystem.

The interplay between fintech and regulatory frameworks is a critical aspect of the evolution of the financial landscape. As fintech companies push the boundaries of innovation, regulatory bodies must adapt to ensure that these advancements do not compromise financial stability or consumer protection. The regulatory environment for fintech varies significantly across different jurisdictions, reflecting diverse approaches to balancing innovation with oversight.

In the United States, for example, regulatory bodies such as the Securities and Exchange Commission (SEC) and the Office of the Comptroller of the Currency (OCC) have taken steps to address the unique challenges posed by fintech. The SEC has issued guidelines on initial coin offerings (ICOs) and digital asset securities, while the OCC has explored the possibility of granting special-purpose national bank charters to fintech companies. These initiatives aim to provide a clear regulatory framework that supports innovation while protecting investors and consumers.

In Europe, the regulatory landscape for fintech is shaped by the European Union's (EU) harmonized regulatory framework. The EU's Revised Payment Services Directive (PSD2) has been a game-changer for the fintech industry, mandating that banks open their payment services and customer data to third-party providers through application programming interfaces (APIs). This has fostered greater competition and innovation in the payments industry, enabling fintech companies to offer new and enhanced services to consumers.

China has emerged as a global leader in fintech, driven by a combination of technological innovation, supportive regulatory policies, and high levels of digital adoption. The Chinese government has actively encouraged the development of fintech, particularly in the areas of mobile payments and digital lending. Companies like Alibaba's Ant Group and Tencent's

WeChat Pay have become dominant players in the Chinese financial ecosystem, offering a wide range of financial services through their digital platforms. However, as the fintech sector has grown, Chinese regulators have also introduced measures to mitigate risks, such as tighter regulations on peer-to-peer lending and increased scrutiny of digital payments.

In developing countries, fintech has played a crucial role in advancing financial inclusion. Regulatory approaches in these regions often focus on creating an enabling environment for fintech to thrive while addressing the unique challenges of reaching underserved populations. For instance, the regulatory framework for mobile money services in Kenya, which supports the widespread use of M-Pesa, has been instrumental in expanding access to financial services for millions of people who previously lacked access to traditional banking.

The evolution of fintech is also closely tied to the development of digital identities and authentication mechanisms. As financial services become increasingly digital, the need for secure and reliable identification methods has become paramount. Biometric authentication, such as fingerprint and facial recognition, has gained traction as a means of enhancing security and convenience. Digital identity solutions, such as India's Aadhaar system, provide a foundation for delivering a wide range of financial services to individuals, particularly in remote and underserved areas.

The integration of artificial intelligence (AI) and machine learning into fintech has further transformed the financial services industry. AI-powered chatbots and virtual assistants are now commonplace in customer service, providing instant support and personalized recommendations. Machine learning algorithms are used to detect fraudulent activities, assess credit risk, and optimize investment strategies. These technologies enable financial institutions to operate more efficiently and make data-driven decisions that enhance the customer experience.

Another significant development in fintech is the rise of neobanks, also known as digital-only banks. Neobanks operate entirely online without physical branches, offering a range of banking services through mobile apps and websites. These banks leverage technology to provide a seamless and user-friendly banking experience, often with lower fees and higher interest rates compared to traditional banks. Neobanks like Revolut, N26, and Chime have attracted millions of customers worldwide, particularly among tech-savvy and younger demographics.

The proliferation of fintech has also led to the emergence of new forms of digital assets and financial instruments. Cryptocurrencies, stablecoins, and tokenized assets represent a new frontier in finance, offering novel ways to store and transfer value. Stablecoins, which are digital currencies pegged to traditional fiat currencies or other assets, aim to combine the benefits of cryptocurrencies with the stability of traditional money. Tokenization, the process of converting real-world assets into digital tokens on a blockchain, has the potential to revolutionize the trading and ownership of assets such as real estate, art, and commodities.

As the fintech landscape continues to evolve, collaboration between traditional financial institutions and fintech companies has become increasingly common. Banks and other established financial entities are partnering with fintech startups to leverage their technological capabilities and innovative solutions. These collaborations enable traditional institutions to enhance their service offerings, improve operational efficiency, and stay competitive in a rapidly changing market. At the same time, fintech companies benefit from the established customer base, regulatory expertise, and financial resources of their traditional counterparts.

The rise of fintech has also prompted a rethinking of financial education and literacy. As financial services become more complex and digital, there is a growing need to equip individuals with the knowledge and skills to navigate this new landscape. Financial literacy programs, both online and offline, are essential in helping consumers understand and effectively use fintech products and services. This is particularly important in promoting responsible financial behavior and protecting consumers from potential risks associated with digital finance.

The integration of environmental, social, and governance (ESG) considerations into fintech is an emerging trend that reflects the broader shift towards sustainable finance. Fintech companies are increasingly incorporating ESG factors into their business models, product offerings, and investment strategies. For example, some fintech platforms enable users to invest in sustainable projects or track the carbon footprint of their spending. This alignment with ESG principles not only addresses the growing demand for socially responsible finance but also contributes to the long-term sustainability of the financial system.

The global impact of fintech is evident in the way it has reshaped financial markets, influenced regulatory policies, and transformed consumer behavior. The continued evolution of fintech will be driven by advances in technology, changing consumer expectations, and the dynamic regulatory environment. As fintech matures, it will likely integrate more deeply with other sectors, such as healthcare, education, and transportation, creating new opportunities and challenges at the intersection of finance and technology.

1.3 An Overview of Central Bank Digital Currencies

The emergence of Central Bank Digital Currencies (CBDCs)

represents a groundbreaking development in the world of finance, reflecting a concerted effort by central banks to adapt to the digital age. CBDCs are digital forms of a country's sovereign currency, issued and regulated by the central bank. Unlike cryptocurrencies such as Bitcoin and Ethereum, which are decentralized and operate independently of any central authority, CBDCs are centralized and backed by the state. This distinction is crucial as it positions CBDCs as a secure and stable medium of exchange within the existing monetary framework.

The rationale behind the development of CBDCs is multifaceted, encompassing goals related to financial inclusion, payment efficiency, monetary policy, and economic stability. Understanding these motivations is essential to grasp the full significance of CBDCs and their potential impact on the global financial system.

1.3.1 Motivation and Goals

One of the primary motivations for developing CBDCs is to enhance financial inclusion. Despite the widespread availability of digital financial services, a significant portion of the global population remains unbanked or underbanked. This is particularly true in developing countries where access to traditional banking infrastructure is limited. CBDCs can provide a more inclusive financial system by offering digital payment solutions that do not require a traditional bank account. This can empower individuals in remote or underserved regions, enabling them to participate in the formal economy and access financial services.

Improving payment efficiency is another critical goal of CBDCs. Traditional payment systems, especially for cross-border transactions, are often slow, expensive, and opaque. CBDCs have the potential to streamline these processes, reducing transaction costs and settlement times while increasing transparency. This efficiency can significantly benefit businesses and consumers, fostering greater economic activity and integration.

CBDCs can also enhance the effectiveness of monetary policy. Central banks use various tools to influence economic activity and maintain price stability, such as interest rates and reserve requirements. However, these tools can be blunt and indirect. With CBDCs, central banks can have a more direct impact on money supply and demand. For instance, they could implement programmable money with specific attributes, such as expiration dates or spending limits, to encourage or discourage certain economic behaviors.

Furthermore, CBDCs can play a role in maintaining financial stability. The introduction of CBDCs could mitigate some of the risks associated with the proliferation of private cryptocurrencies and stablecoins. By offering a state-backed digital currency, central banks can provide a safer alternative that mitigates the risks of financial instability and illicit activities associated with unregulated digital currencies.

1.3.2 Types of CBDCs

CBDCs can be broadly categorized into two types: retail CBDCs and wholesale CBDCs. Each type serves different purposes and targets distinct segments of the financial system.

Retail CBDCs are designed for general public use. They are digital equivalents of cash and can be used for everyday transactions by individuals and businesses. Retail CBDCs aim to enhance financial inclusion, improve payment efficiency, and provide a secure digital alternative to physical cash. By offering a digital form of money that is accessible to everyone, retail CBDCs can facilitate the shift towards a cashless society and reduce the costs associated with printing, distributing, and handling physical currency.

Wholesale CBDCs, on the other hand, are intended for use

by financial institutions, such as banks and payment service providers. These CBDCs are used for large-scale transactions and interbank settlements, aiming to improve the efficiency and security of wholesale payment systems. Wholesale CBDCs can enhance liquidity management, reduce counterparty risks, and streamline cross-border transactions by providing a secure and efficient means of transferring large sums of money.

1.3.3 Technological Foundations

The technological foundation of CBDCs is a critical aspect that determines their functionality, security, and scalability. Blockchain and distributed ledger technologies (DLTs) are often associated with CBDCs due to their potential to provide a secure and transparent infrastructure. However, not all CBDCs are based on blockchain. Central banks can choose from a variety of technological architectures, each with its advantages and trade-offs.

Blockchain-based CBDCs leverage the decentralized and immutable nature of blockchain to ensure transaction security and transparency. This approach can enhance trust and reduce the risk of fraud and tampering. Smart contracts, which are self-executing contracts with the terms of the agreement directly written into code, can also be used to automate complex transactions and enforce compliance with regulatory requirements.

However, blockchain-based systems can face challenges related to scalability and transaction speed. To address these issues, some central banks are exploring hybrid architectures that combine elements of blockchain with traditional centralized systems. These hybrid models aim to provide the benefits of blockchain, such as security and transparency, while maintaining the efficiency and scalability of centralized systems.

1.3.4 Design Choices and Trade-offs

The design of a CBDC involves several critical choices that can significantly impact its functionality and adoption. These design choices include decisions related to access, privacy, programmability, and interoperability.

Access refers to who can use the CBDC and how they can access it. Central banks can choose between providing direct access to individuals and businesses or offering indirect access through intermediaries, such as commercial banks and payment service providers. Direct access can enhance financial inclusion and reduce reliance on intermediaries, but it also requires central banks to manage a larger number of accounts and transactions. Indirect access, on the other hand, leverages the existing financial infrastructure and reduces the operational burden on central banks, but it may limit the inclusivity and reach of the CBDC.

Privacy is another critical consideration. While CBDCs can offer greater transparency in transactions, this transparency must be balanced with the need to protect individual privacy. Central banks must decide how much transaction information should be visible to the public, regulators, and other stakeholders. Ensuring robust privacy protections is essential to maintaining trust and preventing misuse of transaction data.

Programmability refers to the ability to embed specific features and rules into the CBDC. For example, central banks can program CBDCs with expiration dates to encourage spending or set limits on how and where the currency can be used. Programmable money can provide central banks with more precise tools for implementing monetary policy and encouraging desired economic behaviors. However, programmability also introduces complexity and potential risks related to misuse and errors in the programming logic.

Interoperability is crucial for ensuring that CBDCs can seamlessly integrate with existing financial systems and other digital currencies. Central banks must design CBDCs to be compatible with various payment systems, both domestically and internationally. Interoperability can facilitate cross-border transactions, reduce fragmentation in the financial system, and enhance the overall efficiency of digital payments.

1.3.5 Implementation Challenges

The implementation of CBDCs is a complex and multifaceted process that involves addressing various technical, operational, and regulatory challenges. One of the foremost concerns is the impact on financial stability. The introduction of CBDCs could disrupt traditional banking models, as individuals and businesses might prefer holding digital currency directly with the central bank rather than in commercial bank accounts. This could lead to disintermediation, where banks lose their role as intermediaries in the financial system, potentially reducing their capacity to lend and manage liquidity.

Ensuring robust cybersecurity measures is paramount to safeguarding CBDCs against digital threats. Cyberattacks, data breaches, and other security incidents could undermine trust in the digital currency and pose significant risks to the financial system. Central banks must invest in advanced security technologies and protocols to protect the integrity and confidentiality of CBDC transactions.

Regulatory frameworks must evolve to address the unique characteristics of CBDCs. This includes establishing clear guidelines for anti-money laundering (AML) and counter-terrorism financing (CTF) measures, as well as ensuring compliance with data protection and privacy regulations. Collaboration between central banks, financial regulators, and other stakeholders is essential to develop a comprehensive regulatory approach that supports the safe and effective use of CBDCs.

The global significance of CBDCs extends beyond national

borders. The introduction of CBDCs by major economies can have ripple effects across the global financial system. For example, the adoption of a digital yuan by China has sparked discussions about the potential for CBDCs to shift the balance of economic power and influence international trade dynamics. Similarly, the European Central Bank's exploration of a digital euro reflects the growing recognition of CBDCs' strategic importance in maintaining monetary sovereignty and competitiveness.

The exploration of cross-border CBDC arrangements is an emerging area of interest. Central banks are collaborating on initiatives to enable seamless cross-border transactions using CBDCs. These arrangements can reduce the costs and complexities associated with international payments, enhance financial connectivity, and support global economic integration. However, they also require harmonized regulatory frameworks and technological standards to ensure interoperability and security.

As we delve deeper into the landscape of CBDCs, it is essential to consider the diverse approaches taken by different countries. Each nation's economic, political, and social context shapes its strategy for developing and implementing a digital currency. For instance, China's digital yuan project is part of a broader effort to increase digital infrastructure and reduce reliance on the traditional banking system. In contrast, the European Central Bank's digital euro initiative emphasizes maintaining monetary sovereignty and enhancing payment efficiency within the eurozone.

The journey of understanding CBDCs involves navigating complex terrains of technology, economics, and policy. This exploration will provide insights into how CBDCs can be effectively integrated into the existing financial framework while addressing the challenges that accompany their adoption. By examining current developments and future trends, we aim to offer a comprehensive understanding of how Central Bank Digital Currencies will reshape the global financial system, illuminating the path forward in this exciting new era of digital money.

1.4 Case Studies: Early Adopters and Pilot Programs

The journey towards the implementation of Central Bank Digital Currencies (CBDCs) has seen various countries exploring, experimenting, and piloting different models to understand their feasibility, impact, and potential benefits. These early adopters and pilot programs offer valuable insights into the practical challenges and opportunities associated with CBDCs. In this section, we will examine several prominent case studies that highlight the diverse approaches and lessons learned from these pioneering efforts.

1.4.1 THE DIGITAL YUAN: CHINA'S PIONEERING EFFORT

China's digital yuan, officially known as the Digital Currency Electronic Payment (DCEP), represents one of the most advanced and ambitious CBDC projects globally. Spearheaded by the People's Bank of China (PBOC), the digital yuan aims to modernize the country's financial system, enhance payment efficiency, and assert China's dominance in the global digital economy.

The development of the digital yuan began in earnest in 2014, with the PBOC establishing a dedicated research institute to explore the feasibility and implications of a national digital currency. Over the years, the project has undergone extensive research, development, and testing phases, culminating in a series of large-scale pilot programs across multiple cities.

The digital yuan operates on a two-tiered system. In the first tier, the PBOC issues the digital currency to commercial banks and other authorized financial institutions. In the second tier, these institutions distribute the digital yuan to the public through various channels, including mobile apps and digital wallets. This system leverages the existing financial infrastructure, ensuring a smooth transition from traditional to digital currency.

The pilot programs for the digital yuan have been extensive, involving millions of users and thousands of businesses. These pilots have been conducted in major cities such as Shenzhen, Suzhou, and Chengdu, as well as during high-profile events like the 2022 Winter Olympics in Beijing. Participants have used the digital yuan for a wide range of transactions, including retail purchases, bill payments, and transportation fares.

One of the key objectives of the digital yuan is to enhance financial inclusion. By providing a digital alternative to cash, the PBOC aims to reach unbanked and underbanked populations, particularly in rural areas. The digital yuan can be accessed through mobile phones, making it a convenient and accessible payment method for those without traditional bank accounts.

The pilot programs have also focused on improving payment efficiency and reducing transaction costs. The digital yuan facilitates instant, low-cost transactions, both domestically and internationally. This has significant implications for cross-border trade and remittances, where traditional payment systems often involve high fees and lengthy settlement times.

However, the digital yuan project has not been without challenges. Ensuring the security and privacy of transactions is a critical concern, given the potential for cyberattacks and data breaches. The PBOC has implemented robust encryption and authentication measures to safeguard the digital currency, but ongoing vigilance is required to address emerging threats.

1.4.2 THE SAND DOLLAR: THE BAHAMAS 'DIGITAL CURRENCY

The Bahamas has been a trailblazer in the development and deployment of CBDCs with its digital currency known as the

Sand Dollar. Launched by the Central Bank of The Bahamas in October 2020, the Sand Dollar is one of the first fully operational retail CBDCs in the world.

The motivation behind the Sand Dollar project is rooted in the unique geographical and economic challenges faced by The Bahamas. The archipelago comprises numerous islands, many of which are remote and lack adequate banking infrastructure. The Sand Dollar aims to enhance financial inclusion by providing residents with a secure and convenient digital payment solution.

The Sand Dollar operates on a centralized infrastructure managed by the Central Bank of The Bahamas. It can be accessed through digital wallets on mobile phones, allowing users to make transactions, transfer funds, and store value digitally. The digital currency is backed 1:1 by the Bahamian dollar, ensuring its stability and trustworthiness.

The implementation of the Sand Dollar involved a phased approach, starting with pilot programs on the islands of Exuma and Abaco. These pilots provided valuable insights into user behavior, technical requirements, and potential challenges. Following the successful pilots, the Sand Dollar was rolled out nationwide, making it accessible to all residents and businesses.

One of the notable features of the Sand Dollar is its focus on interoperability. The digital currency can be seamlessly integrated with existing financial systems and payment platforms, enabling users to conduct transactions across different channels. This interoperability enhances the usability and adoption of the Sand Dollar, making it a versatile tool for various financial activities.

The Sand Dollar has also been designed with robust security and privacy measures. The Central Bank of The Bahamas employs advanced encryption and authentication technologies to protect users' data and ensure the integrity of transactions.

Additionally, the digital currency incorporates features to comply with anti-money laundering (AML) and counter-terrorism financing (CTF) regulations, further enhancing its security framework.

1.4.3 THE DIGITAL EURO: THE EUROPEAN CENTRAL BANK'S EXPLORATION

The European Central Bank (ECB) has been actively exploring the development of a digital euro, reflecting the growing interest in CBDCs among advanced economies. The digital euro project aims to complement the existing euro currency, providing a digital alternative that enhances payment efficiency and supports financial stability.

The ECB's exploration of the digital euro involves extensive research, consultation, and experimentation. In October 2020, the ECB published a comprehensive report outlining the potential benefits and challenges of a digital euro. The report highlighted key areas of focus, including payment efficiency, financial inclusion, monetary policy, and legal considerations.

One of the primary motivations for the digital euro is to improve payment efficiency in the eurozone. The digital euro aims to facilitate instant, low-cost transactions, reducing the reliance on cash and traditional payment methods. This efficiency is particularly relevant in the context of cross-border payments, where existing systems can be slow and expensive.

Financial inclusion is another important goal of the digital euro. By providing a digital payment solution accessible to all residents of the eurozone, the ECB aims to reach unbanked and underbanked populations. The digital euro can be accessed through various channels, including mobile apps and digital wallets, making it a convenient option for individuals and businesses.

The ECB has also emphasized the potential of the digital euro to enhance monetary policy. By providing a digital form of central bank money, the ECB can have greater control over money supply and demand. The digital euro can be designed with features that support monetary policy objectives, such as negative interest rates or limits on holdings.

The exploration of the digital euro involves extensive engagement with stakeholders, including financial institutions, technology providers, and the public. The ECB has launched public consultations and conducted technical trials to gather feedback and assess the feasibility of the digital euro. These efforts are aimed at ensuring that the digital euro meets the needs of users while addressing potential challenges and risks.

1.4.4 PROJECT UBIN: SINGAPORE'S WHOLESALE CBDC INITIATIVE

Singapore has been at the forefront of financial innovation, and its wholesale CBDC initiative, known as Project Ubin, is a testament to this commitment. Launched by the Monetary Authority of Singapore (MAS), Project Ubin explores the use of blockchain and distributed ledger technology (DLT) for interbank payments and settlements.

Project Ubin aims to improve the efficiency, security, and transparency of Singapore's financial infrastructure. The initiative involves collaboration between the MAS, financial institutions, and technology providers to develop and test a blockchain-based interbank payment system.

The project has been conducted in multiple phases, each focusing on different aspects of the wholesale CBDC system. In the initial phases, the project explored the feasibility of using DLT for interbank payments, examining issues related to transaction speed, scalability, and security. Subsequent phases expanded the scope to include cross-border payments and the integration of other financial services.

One of the key achievements of Project Ubin is the development of a blockchain-based prototype for interbank settlements. This prototype demonstrated the potential of DLT to streamline the clearing and settlement process, reducing the time and costs associated with traditional systems. The project also highlighted the benefits of enhanced transparency and traceability in financial transactions.

Project Ubin has garnered international attention and collaboration. The MAS has partnered with central banks and financial institutions from other countries to explore cross-border payment solutions using blockchain technology. These collaborations aim to create a more interconnected and efficient global financial system.

The success of Project Ubin has paved the way for further exploration and development of wholesale CBDCs in Singapore. The MAS continues to engage with stakeholders and leverage technological advancements to enhance the country's financial infrastructure.

1.4.5 SWEDEN'S E-KRONA: ADVANCING TOWARDS A CASHLESS SOCIETY

Sweden, known for its progressive approach to technology and finance, has been exploring the development of a retail CBDC known as the e-krona. The Riksbank, Sweden's central bank, initiated the e-krona project in response to the declining use of cash and the increasing popularity of digital payments.

The e-krona aims to provide a digital complement to cash, ensuring that the public continues to have access to central bank money in a digital age. The Riksbank envisions the e-krona as a secure, efficient, and accessible payment solution that supports the country's transition towards a cashless society.

The exploration of the e-krona involves extensive research, experimentation, and stakeholder engagement. The Riksbank has conducted several pilot programs to test the technical and operational aspects of the e-krona. These pilots have focused on issues such as transaction speed, security, user experience, and interoperability with existing payment systems.

One of the notable features of the e-krona project is its emphasis on inclusivity. The Riksbank aims to ensure that the e-krona is accessible to all residents, including those who may not have access to traditional banking services. The digital currency can be used for a wide range of transactions, from everyday purchases to peer-to-peer payments, providing a versatile and user-friendly payment option.

The e-krona project also explores the potential impact on monetary policy and financial stability. By providing a digital form of central bank money, the Riksbank can enhance its ability to implement monetary policy and monitor money supply. The e-krona can also provide a safe and stable alternative to private digital currencies, reducing the risks associated with unregulated digital assets.

The lessons learned from Sweden's e-krona project have significant implications for other countries exploring the development of retail CBDCs. The Riksbank's emphasis on accessibility, security, and user experience provides a valuable framework for designing and implementing digital currencies that meet the needs of the public.

These case studies highlight the diverse approaches and motivations behind the development of CBDCs. From enhancing financial inclusion and payment efficiency to supporting monetary policy and financial stability, the early adopters and pilot programs offer valuable insights into the potential benefits and challenges of digital currencies. As more countries explore the possibilities of CBDCs, these experiences will provide a foundation for understanding how digital currencies can be effectively integrated into the global financial system.

CHAPTER 2: IMPACT OF CBDCS ON GLOBAL TRADE

2.1 Enhancing Trade Efficiency and Transparency

Central Bank Digital Currencies (CBDCs) hold the potential to significantly transform global trade by enhancing efficiency and transparency. The intricate web of international trade involves numerous stakeholders, including exporters, importers, banks, payment service providers, and regulatory authorities. Traditional trade finance processes are often plagued by inefficiencies, delays, and high costs, which can hinder the smooth flow of goods and services across borders. CBDCs can address these issues by providing a more streamlined, secure, and transparent framework for conducting international transactions.

2.1.1 REDUCING TRANSACTION COSTS AND SETTLEMENT TIMES

One of the most immediate benefits of CBDCs in the context of global trade is the reduction of transaction costs and settlement times. Traditional cross-border payments involve multiple intermediaries, such as correspondent banks, which add layers of complexity and cost to the process. Each intermediary charges fees for its services, and the involvement of multiple parties can lead to delays in settlement, sometimes taking several days to complete a transaction.

CBDCs can streamline this process by enabling direct transfers between central banks and financial institutions, bypassing the need for correspondent banks. This can significantly reduce the costs associated with cross-border payments, making international trade more affordable for businesses of all sizes. Furthermore, the use of blockchain and distributed ledger technology (DLT) in CBDCs can facilitate real-time or near-real-time settlement of transactions, eliminating the delays inherent in traditional systems.

For example, a transaction using CBDCs could be completed within minutes, as opposed to days, allowing businesses to expedite the receipt of payments and improve cash flow management. This efficiency can be particularly beneficial for small and medium-sized enterprises (SMEs), which often face greater challenges in accessing trade finance and managing liquidity.

2.1.2 ENHANCING TRANSPARENCY AND REDUCING FRAUD

Transparency is a critical factor in international trade, where the movement of goods and funds across borders must be carefully tracked and verified. Traditional trade finance processes often lack transparency, making it difficult to trace the flow of funds and detect fraudulent activities. The complexity and opacity of these processes can also lead to disputes between trading partners, further complicating trade relationships.

CBDCs can enhance transparency by providing a secure and immutable record of transactions on a blockchain or distributed ledger. Each transaction is recorded in a transparent and tamper-proof manner, allowing all parties involved to verify the authenticity and integrity of the transaction. This transparency can help reduce the risk of fraud and ensure that funds are used for their intended purposes.

In addition, the use of smart contracts—self-executing

contracts with the terms of the agreement directly written into code—can further enhance transparency and efficiency in trade finance. Smart contracts can automate various aspects of trade transactions, such as payment releases upon the fulfillment of certain conditions (e.g., delivery of goods, submission of shipping documents). This automation reduces the need for manual intervention, minimizes errors, and ensures that transactions are executed according to predefined rules.

For instance, in a cross-border trade transaction, a smart contract could automatically release payment to the exporter once the goods have been delivered and verified by a trusted third party. This not only streamlines the payment process but also provides both parties with greater assurance that the terms of the trade agreement will be honored.

2.1.3 FACILITATING CROSS-BORDER TRADE INTEGRATION

CBDCs have the potential to facilitate greater integration of cross-border trade by harmonizing payment systems and reducing barriers to entry. The current global trade environment is characterized by a patchwork of payment systems and regulatory frameworks, which can create friction and increase the cost of doing business internationally. This lack of standardization can be particularly challenging for SMEs and businesses operating in emerging markets.

By providing a standardized and interoperable digital currency, CBDCs can help bridge these gaps and create a more cohesive global trade ecosystem. Central banks and regulatory authorities can collaborate to establish common standards and protocols for CBDC transactions, ensuring that digital currencies are compatible across different jurisdictions. This harmonization can simplify the process of conducting cross-border trade, making it easier for businesses to expand their operations and reach new markets.

Moreover, CBDCs can enhance financial inclusion by providing businesses in emerging markets with access to secure and efficient payment solutions. In many developing countries, traditional banking infrastructure is limited, and businesses often rely on informal and costly methods for cross-border transactions. CBDCs can offer a formal, low-cost alternative that enables businesses to participate more fully in the global economy.

For example, a small business in a developing country could use a CBDC to pay suppliers in another country, bypassing the need for expensive and unreliable remittance services. The use of CBDCs can also facilitate greater access to trade finance, as financial institutions can more easily assess the creditworthiness of businesses based on their transaction histories recorded on the blockchain.

2.1.4 STRENGTHENING REGULATORY OVERSIGHT AND COMPLIANCE

Regulatory compliance is a critical aspect of international trade, where businesses must adhere to various laws and regulations related to anti-money laundering (AML), counter-terrorism financing (CTF), and sanctions. Ensuring compliance with these regulations can be complex and time-consuming, particularly for businesses operating in multiple jurisdictions.

CBDCs can enhance regulatory oversight and compliance by providing regulators with greater visibility into cross-border transactions. The transparent and auditable nature of blockchain technology allows regulators to monitor transactions in real-time, identify suspicious activities, and enforce compliance with AML and CTF regulations. This increased transparency can help prevent illicit activities and ensure that the global trade system operates with integrity.

Furthermore, the programmability of CBDCs can enable the implementation of automated compliance checks and controls. For example, smart contracts can be designed to automatically flag transactions that exceed certain thresholds or involve high-risk jurisdictions, triggering additional scrutiny or reporting requirements. This automation reduces the administrative burden on businesses and ensures that compliance measures are consistently applied.

In addition to enhancing regulatory oversight, CBDCs can also support the enforcement of international trade agreements and sanctions. By providing a digital record of transactions, CBDCs can help ensure that businesses adhere to the terms of trade agreements and that sanctioned entities are prevented from engaging in prohibited activities. This strengthens the rule of law in international trade and promotes fair and transparent business practices.

2.1.5 CASE STUDY: THE BANK OF INTERNATIONAL SETTLEMENTS (BIS) INNOVATION HUB

The Bank of International Settlements (BIS) Innovation Hub has been at the forefront of exploring the potential of CBDCs to enhance trade efficiency and transparency. The BIS Innovation Hub collaborates with central banks and other stakeholders to conduct research, pilot projects, and develop innovative solutions for the global financial system.

One notable initiative is Project Inthanon-LionRock, a collaboration between the Bank of Thailand and the Hong Kong Monetary Authority. This project explores the use of CBDCs for cross-border payments and trade finance, leveraging blockchain technology to streamline transactions and reduce settlement times. The pilot demonstrated the feasibility of using CBDCs to facilitate real-time cross-border payments, significantly reducing the time and cost associated with traditional methods.

Another example is Project Dunbar, a collaboration between the BIS Innovation Hub and several central banks, including the Reserve Bank of Australia and the Monetary Authority of Singapore. Project Dunbar aims to develop a multi-CBDC platform for international settlements, enabling central banks to transact directly with each other using digital currencies. This platform has the potential to enhance the efficiency and transparency of cross-border trade by providing a secure and standardized infrastructure for CBDC transactions.

These case studies highlight the potential of CBDCs to revolutionize global trade by enhancing efficiency, transparency, and regulatory oversight. As more central banks explore and implement CBDCs, the lessons learned from these initiatives will provide valuable insights into how digital currencies can be effectively integrated into the global trade ecosystem.

The transformation of global trade through CBDCs is not without challenges. Ensuring interoperability, addressing privacy concerns, and managing the impact on traditional financial systems are critical considerations that must be addressed. However, the potential benefits of CBDCs in enhancing trade efficiency and transparency are significant, offering a promising path towards a more integrated and efficient global economy.

As we move forward, the continued exploration and development of CBDCs will play a crucial role in shaping the future of global trade. By leveraging the power of digital currencies, we can create a more inclusive, efficient, and transparent trade environment that benefits businesses and consumers worldwide.

2.2 Reducing Transaction Costs and Cross-Border Payments

The current landscape of cross-border payments is fraught with inefficiencies, high costs, and delays, which can significantly hinder international trade and economic integration. Central Bank Digital Currencies (CBDCs) offer a transformative solution by streamlining the process, reducing transaction costs, and accelerating settlement times. This section delves into the mechanisms by which CBDCs can achieve these improvements and examines the potential impact on global commerce.

Cross-border payments are essential for international trade, investment, and remittances. However, traditional cross-border payment systems are notoriously slow, costly, and complex. These challenges stem from several factors, including the involvement of multiple intermediaries, differences in national payment infrastructures, regulatory requirements, and currency conversion processes.

The traditional correspondent banking model is a primary contributor to these inefficiencies. In this model, payments must pass through a network of correspondent banks, each of which charges fees and adds layers of processing time. This can result in high costs for businesses and consumers, particularly for smaller transactions where fees represent a significant percentage of the transaction amount. Additionally, the need to navigate different time zones and banking hours can cause delays, often taking several days for payments to be settled.

Currency conversion is another significant hurdle in cross-border payments. The process of exchanging one currency for another involves not only conversion fees but also the risk of fluctuating exchange rates. Businesses must manage this risk, which can add to the overall cost and complexity of international transactions.

CBDCs have the potential to address many of the inefficiencies associated with cross-border payments by providing a more streamlined, cost-effective, and transparent solution. By leveraging blockchain and distributed ledger technology (DLT), CBDCs can facilitate direct, peer-to-peer transactions between central banks and financial institutions, bypassing the need for multiple intermediaries.

One of the key advantages of CBDCs is their ability to

provide real-time or near-real-time settlement of transactions. Blockchain-based systems can process and verify transactions almost instantaneously, significantly reducing the time it takes for payments to be settled. This speed not only improves cash flow for businesses but also reduces the risk associated with delayed payments.

For example, in a traditional cross-border transaction, an exporter may have to wait several days to receive payment from an importer due to the various intermediaries involved in the process. With CBDCs, the payment can be made directly from the importer's bank to the exporter's bank in a matter of minutes, ensuring that the funds are available more quickly.

The reduction of transaction costs is one of the most compelling benefits of CBDCs in cross-border payments. By eliminating the need for correspondent banks and other intermediaries, CBDCs can drastically reduce the fees associated with international transactions. This cost saving can be particularly beneficial for small and medium-sized enterprises (SMEs), which often face higher relative costs for cross-border payments compared to larger corporations.

Moreover, the transparency and efficiency of blockchain technology can reduce operational costs for financial institutions. The automated and secure nature of blockchain transactions minimizes the need for manual processing and reconciliation, lowering administrative expenses. Additionally, the use of smart contracts can further streamline processes by automating the execution of payment terms and conditions.

For instance, in a cross-border trade transaction, a smart contract could automatically release payment to the exporter once the goods have been delivered and verified, without the need for manual intervention. This not only reduces the time and cost associated with payment processing but also provides greater assurance to both parties that the transaction will be executed as agreed.

Transparency is a critical factor in cross-border payments, where the movement of funds across borders must be carefully monitored to prevent fraud, money laundering, and other illicit activities. Traditional payment systems often lack transparency, making it difficult to trace the flow of funds and ensure compliance with regulatory requirements.

CBDCs can enhance transparency by providing a secure and immutable record of transactions on a blockchain or distributed ledger. Each transaction is recorded in a transparent and tamper-proof manner, allowing regulators, financial institutions, and businesses to verify the authenticity and integrity of the transaction. This transparency can help reduce the risk of fraud and ensure that funds are used for their intended purposes.

In addition, the use of CBDCs can enhance security by reducing the reliance on vulnerable legacy systems. Blockchain technology provides a robust security framework that is resistant to hacking and tampering. The decentralized nature of blockchain ensures that there is no single point of failure, making it more difficult for malicious actors to compromise the system.

CASE STUDIES AND PILOT PROJECTS

Several central banks and financial institutions around the world are exploring the use of CBDCs for cross-border payments through pilot projects and collaborative initiatives. These efforts provide valuable insights into the potential benefits and challenges of implementing CBDCs for international transactions.

One notable example is the m-CBDC Bridge Project, a collaboration between the Hong Kong Monetary Authority, the Bank of Thailand, the Central Bank of the United Arab Emirates, and the People's Bank of China. This project aims to develop a cross-border payment system using multiple CBDCs, leveraging blockchain technology to enable real-time, low-cost transactions between participating countries.

The m-CBDC Bridge Project has demonstrated the feasibility of using CBDCs to facilitate cross-border payments, significantly reducing transaction times and costs compared to traditional methods. The pilot has also highlighted the importance of interoperability and collaboration between central banks to ensure that different CBDC systems can work seamlessly together.

Another example is Project Jasper-Ubin, a joint initiative between the Bank of Canada and the Monetary Authority of Singapore. This project explored the use of DLT for cross-border payments and settlements, focusing on enhancing efficiency and reducing the risks associated with traditional correspondent banking. The pilot demonstrated that DLT could streamline the settlement process, providing a faster and more cost-effective solution for cross-border transactions.

The adoption of CBDCs for cross-border payments holds significant promise for transforming the global financial landscape. By providing a more efficient, cost-effective, and transparent solution, CBDCs can enhance the competitiveness of businesses, support economic integration, and promote financial inclusion.

However, the successful implementation of CBDCs for cross-border payments requires careful consideration of several factors. Ensuring interoperability between different CBDC systems is crucial to facilitating seamless transactions across borders. Central banks and financial institutions must collaborate to establish common standards and protocols, enabling CBDCs to function harmoniously within the global financial system.

Additionally, addressing regulatory and compliance challenges is essential to maintaining the integrity and security of cross-border payments. Clear guidelines and frameworks must be established to prevent illicit activities and ensure that CBDCs adhere to international regulatory standards.

2.3 CBDCs and International Trade Agreements

The integration of Central Bank Digital Currencies (CBDCs) into international trade agreements represents a significant evolution in the global economic landscape. CBDCs have the potential to streamline and enhance the efficiency of international trade, providing a more secure and transparent framework for cross-border transactions. This section explores how CBDCs can be incorporated into international trade agreements, the benefits they offer, and the challenges that need to be addressed.

2.3.1 The Role of CBDCs in International Trade

International trade agreements are designed to facilitate the flow of goods, services, and capital across borders by establishing rules and standards that govern trade relations between countries. These agreements aim to reduce trade barriers, promote economic cooperation, and ensure fair competition. The introduction of CBDCs can further enhance the objectives of international trade agreements by providing a modernized and efficient payment infrastructure.

CBDCs can simplify the process of cross-border payments, reducing the reliance on multiple intermediaries and minimizing the risks associated with currency conversion and fluctuations. By providing a direct and transparent means of transferring value between countries, CBDCs can support the seamless execution of trade agreements and improve the overall efficiency of international trade.

2.3.2 Enhancing Trade Efficiency and Reducing Costs

One of the primary benefits of incorporating CBDCs into international trade agreements is the potential to enhance trade efficiency and reduce costs. Traditional cross-border payments often involve multiple intermediaries, such as correspondent banks, which can lead to delays, increased transaction costs, and complexities in managing different currencies.

CBDCs can address these challenges by enabling direct transfers between central banks and financial institutions, bypassing the need for intermediaries. This can significantly reduce the time and cost associated with cross-border transactions, making international trade more accessible and cost-effective for businesses of all sizes.

For example, a trade agreement between two countries that have implemented CBDCs can specify the use of digital currencies for settling trade-related payments. This can streamline the payment process, reduce the need for currency conversion, and minimize the risks associated with exchange rate fluctuations. By providing a stable and efficient payment infrastructure, CBDCs can support the objectives of trade agreements and promote economic integration.

2.3.3 Supporting Transparency and Compliance

Transparency is a critical aspect of international trade agreements, where the movement of goods, services, and funds across borders must be carefully monitored to prevent fraud, money laundering, and other illicit activities. Traditional payment systems often lack transparency, making it difficult to trace the flow of funds and ensure compliance with regulatory requirements.

CBDCs can enhance transparency by providing a secure and immutable record of transactions on a blockchain or distributed ledger. Each transaction is recorded in a transparent and tamper-proof manner, allowing regulators, financial institutions, and businesses to verify the authenticity and integrity of the transaction. This transparency can help reduce the risk of fraud and ensure that funds are used for their intended purposes.

Incorporating CBDCs into international trade agreements can also support compliance with anti-money laundering (AML) and counter-terrorism financing (CTF) regulations. The transparent nature of blockchain technology allows regulators to monitor transactions in real-time, identify suspicious activities, and enforce compliance with AML and CTF measures. This can enhance the integrity of the global trade system and ensure that trade agreements are implemented in a secure and compliant manner.

2.3.4 Facilitating Cross-Border Trade Integration

CBDCs have the potential to facilitate greater integration of cross-border trade by harmonizing payment systems and reducing barriers to entry. The current global trade environment is characterized by a patchwork of payment systems and regulatory frameworks, which can create friction and increase the cost of doing business internationally.

By providing a standardized and interoperable digital currency, CBDCs can help bridge these gaps and create a more cohesive global trade ecosystem. Central banks and regulatory authorities can collaborate to establish common standards and protocols for CBDC transactions, ensuring that digital currencies are compatible across different jurisdictions. This harmonization can simplify the process of conducting cross-border trade, making it easier for businesses to expand their operations and reach new markets.

For instance, a regional trade agreement among countries in a specific economic bloc can include provisions for the use of CBDCs for trade-related payments. By adopting a common digital currency framework, these countries can facilitate seamless transactions, reduce trade barriers, and promote economic cooperation. This can enhance the competitiveness of businesses in the region and support the overall objectives of the trade agreement.

2.3.5 Case Study: The Belt and Road Initiative and Digital Currency Integration

The Belt and Road Initiative (BRI) is a global development strategy adopted by China to enhance trade and economic cooperation across Asia, Europe, and Africa. The initiative involves the development of infrastructure projects, trade corridors, and economic partnerships aimed at promoting connectivity and economic growth.

China's digital yuan, also known as the Digital Currency Electronic Payment (DCEP), has the potential to play a significant role in the BRI by providing a secure and efficient payment solution for cross-border trade. The integration of the digital yuan into BRI-related trade agreements can streamline payment processes, reduce transaction costs, and enhance transparency.

For example, infrastructure projects funded under the BRI can specify the use of the digital yuan for payments to contractors, suppliers, and other stakeholders. This can simplify the payment process, reduce the need for currency conversion, and ensure that funds are transferred in a secure and transparent manner. The use of the digital yuan can also enhance regulatory oversight and compliance, ensuring that BRI projects adhere to international standards and regulations.

The integration of CBDCs into the BRI can serve as a model for other international trade agreements, demonstrating the potential benefits of digital currencies in enhancing trade efficiency and promoting economic cooperation. By leveraging the power of CBDCs, countries can create a more integrated and efficient global trade system that supports sustainable economic growth.

While the potential benefits of incorporating CBDCs into international trade agreements are significant, several challenges and considerations must be addressed to ensure successful implementation. One of the primary challenges is ensuring interoperability between different CBDC systems. Central banks and regulatory authorities must collaborate to establish common standards and protocols that enable seamless transactions across borders.

Addressing privacy and security concerns is also critical. While CBDCs can enhance transparency, it is essential to balance this transparency with the need to protect individual privacy and ensure the security of transactions. Robust encryption and authentication measures must be implemented to safeguard against cyberattacks and data breaches.

Regulatory and legal considerations must also be addressed. The incorporation of CBDCs into international trade agreements requires clear guidelines and frameworks that define the roles and responsibilities of different stakeholders. Ensuring compliance with AML, CTF, and other regulatory requirements is essential to maintaining the integrity of the global trade system.

Finally, managing the impact of CBDCs on traditional financial systems and intermediaries is a critical consideration. The introduction of CBDCs can disrupt existing payment infrastructures and financial institutions, potentially leading to disintermediation and other challenges. Policymakers must carefully assess the potential impact and develop strategies to mitigate any negative effects.

The integration of CBDCs into international trade agreements represents a promising opportunity to enhance the efficiency, transparency, and security of global trade. By leveraging the power of digital currencies, countries can create a more integrated and efficient trade ecosystem that supports economic cooperation and sustainable growth.

2.4 Case Studies: CBDCs in Action Across Global Markets

The development and implementation of Central Bank Digital Currencies (CBDCs) are being actively explored by numerous countries worldwide. These efforts provide invaluable insights into how digital currencies can enhance financial systems, reduce transaction costs, and facilitate international trade. In this section, we will examine several case studies from different global markets to understand the practical applications, benefits, and challenges of CBDCs.

2.4.1 The Digital Yuan: China's Pioneering Initiative

China's digital yuan, officially known as the Digital Currency Electronic Payment (DCEP), is one of the most advanced and widely publicized CBDC projects. Spearheaded by the People's Bank of China (PBOC), the digital yuan aims to modernize the country's payment infrastructure, reduce dependence on cash, and counter the growing influence of private cryptocurrencies.

The PBOC began researching the digital yuan in 2014, and extensive pilot programs have been conducted in major cities such as Shenzhen, Suzhou, and Chengdu. These pilots have involved millions of users and thousands of businesses, focusing on a wide range of transactions, from retail purchases to government services.

The digital yuan operates on a two-tiered system: the PBOC issues the currency to commercial banks and other authorized institutions, which then distribute it to the public. This approach leverages existing financial infrastructure, ensuring a smooth transition to the digital currency.

One of the significant advantages observed during the pilot programs is the reduction in transaction costs. Traditional payment systems in China often involve multiple intermediaries, leading to higher fees and slower transactions. The digital yuan enables direct transactions between parties, reducing the need for intermediaries and lowering costs. Additionally, the transparency and traceability of transactions on the blockchain enhance security and reduce the risk of fraud.

2.4.2 THE SAND DOLLAR: THE BAHAMAS 'DIGITAL CURRENCY

The Bahamas has made significant strides in digital currency innovation with the launch of the Sand Dollar, one of the first fully operational retail CBDCs. The Central Bank of The Bahamas introduced the Sand Dollar in October 2020 to enhance financial inclusion, improve payment efficiency, and modernize the financial system.

The Sand Dollar can be accessed through digital wallets on mobile devices, making it accessible to the unbanked and underbanked populations, particularly in the archipelago's remote islands. The digital currency is backed 1:1 by the Bahamian dollar, ensuring its stability and trustworthiness.

The implementation of the Sand Dollar has demonstrated several key benefits. Firstly, it has significantly reduced the costs associated with cash handling and distribution. The digital currency provides a secure and efficient alternative to physical cash, reducing the reliance on traditional banking infrastructure. Additionally, the Sand Dollar has improved payment efficiency, enabling real-time transactions and reducing settlement times.

2.4.3 E-KRONA: SWEDEN'S DIGITAL CURRENCY INITIATIVE

Sweden, known for its progressive approach to technology and finance, has been exploring the development of a retail CBDC known as the e-krona. The Riksbank, Sweden's central bank, initiated the e-krona project in response to the declining use of cash and the increasing popularity of digital payments.

The e-krona aims to provide a digital complement to cash, ensuring that the public continues to have access to central bank money in a digital age. The Riksbank envisions the e-krona as a secure, efficient, and accessible payment solution that supports the country's transition towards a cashless society.

Pilot programs for the e-krona have focused on testing the technical and operational aspects of the digital currency. These pilots have demonstrated the potential for the e-krona to enhance payment efficiency, reduce transaction costs, and support financial inclusion. The Riksbank has also explored the use of the e-krona for various types of transactions, from retail payments to peer-to-peer transfers.

One of the key findings from the e-krona pilots is the importance of ensuring interoperability with existing payment systems. The Riksbank has emphasized the need for the e-krona to work seamlessly with other digital payment methods, enhancing its usability and adoption.

2.4.4 PROJECT UBIN: SINGAPORE'S WHOLESALE CBDC

Project Ubin is an initiative by the Monetary Authority of Singapore (MAS) that explores the use of blockchain and distributed ledger technology (DLT) for wholesale CBDCs. The project aims to improve the efficiency, security, and transparency of Singapore's financial infrastructure.

Project Ubin has been conducted in multiple phases, each focusing on different aspects of wholesale CBDC systems. The initial phases explored the feasibility of using DLT for interbank payments and settlements, addressing issues related to transaction speed, scalability, and security. Subsequent phases expanded the scope to include cross-border payments and the integration of other financial services.

The project has demonstrated the potential of blockchain technology to streamline the settlement process, reducing the time and costs associated with traditional systems. The use of DLT has also enhanced transparency and traceability, providing a secure framework for financial transactions.

One notable achievement of Project Ubin is the development of a blockchain-based prototype for cross-border payments. This prototype enables real-time, low-cost transactions between participating countries, highlighting the potential for CBDCs to facilitate international trade and economic cooperation.

2.4.5 THE DIGITAL EURO: THE EUROPEAN CENTRAL BANK'S EXPLORATION

The European Central Bank (ECB) has been actively exploring the development of a digital euro, reflecting the growing interest in CBDCs among advanced economies. The digital euro project aims to complement the existing euro currency, providing a digital alternative that enhances payment efficiency and supports financial stability.

The ECB's exploration of the digital euro involves extensive research, consultation, and experimentation. Public consultations and technical trials have been conducted to gather feedback and assess the feasibility of the digital euro. These efforts are aimed at ensuring that the digital euro meets the needs of users while addressing potential challenges and risks.

One of the primary motivations for the digital euro is to improve payment efficiency in the eurozone. The digital euro aims to facilitate instant, low-cost transactions, reducing the reliance on cash and traditional payment methods. This efficiency is particularly relevant in the context of cross-border payments, where existing systems can be slow and expensive.

The ECB has also emphasized the potential of the digital euro to enhance financial inclusion. By providing a digital payment solution accessible to all residents of the eurozone, the ECB aims to reach unbanked and underbanked populations. The digital euro can be accessed through various channels, including mobile apps and digital wallets, making it a convenient option for individuals and businesses.

2.4.6 THE DIGITAL RUPEE: INDIA'S APPROACH TO CBDCS

India, with its large and diverse economy, has also been exploring the potential of CBDCs through the development of the digital rupee. The Reserve Bank of India (RBI) has initiated pilot programs to test the feasibility and implications of a digital currency for enhancing the country's payment infrastructure.

The digital rupee aims to provide a secure and efficient alternative to physical cash, reducing the costs associated with cash handling and distribution. The RBI's pilot programs have focused on various use cases, including retail payments, government disbursements, and cross-border remittances.

One of the key findings from the digital rupee pilots is the potential for CBDCs to enhance financial inclusion. By providing a digital payment solution accessible through mobile devices, the digital rupee can reach unbanked and underbanked populations, particularly in rural areas. This can empower individuals to participate more fully in the formal economy and access a wider range of financial services.

The implementation of the digital rupee has also highlighted the importance of regulatory and security considerations. The RBI has emphasized the need for robust encryption and authentication measures to protect the digital currency from cyber threats and ensure the privacy of transactions.

2.4.7 CROSS-BORDER INITIATIVES: THE M-CBDC BRIDGE PROJECT

The m-CBDC Bridge Project is a collaborative initiative involving multiple central banks, including the Hong Kong Monetary Authority, the Bank of Thailand, the Central Bank of the United

Arab Emirates, and the People's Bank of China. This project aims to develop a cross-border payment system using multiple CBDCs, leveraging blockchain technology to enable real-time, low-cost transactions between participating countries.

The m-CBDC Bridge Project has demonstrated the feasibility of using CBDCs to facilitate cross-border payments, significantly reducing transaction times and costs compared to traditional methods. The pilot has also highlighted the importance of interoperability and collaboration between central banks to ensure that different CBDC systems can work seamlessly together.

The project's success has provided valuable insights into the potential for CBDCs to enhance international trade and economic cooperation. By providing a secure and efficient payment infrastructure, the m-CBDC Bridge Project has shown how digital currencies can support the objectives of international trade agreements and promote economic integration.

These case studies highlight the diverse approaches and motivations behind the development and implementation of CBDCs across global markets. From enhancing payment efficiency and reducing transaction costs to supporting financial inclusion and regulatory compliance, CBDCs offer a wide range of benefits for both domestic and international transactions.

The lessons learned from these early adopters and pilot programs provide valuable insights into the potential of CBDCs to transform the global financial landscape. As more countries explore and implement digital currencies, continued innovation and collaboration will be essential to realizing the full potential of CBDCs in enhancing global trade and economic cooperation.

CHAPTER 3: IMPACT ON INTERNATIONAL INVESTMENT

3.1 CBDCs and Cross-Border Investment Flows

Central Bank Digital Currencies (CBDCs) are poised to revolutionize cross-border investment flows by addressing several longstanding inefficiencies in the global financial system. This section explores how CBDCs can enhance cross-border investment, streamline capital flows, reduce transaction costs, and provide greater transparency and security.

3.1.1 Enhancing Capital Flow Efficiency

Traditional cross-border investment processes are often hampered by multiple layers of intermediaries, varying regulatory environments, and the need for currency conversions. These factors contribute to delays, higher costs, and increased complexity for investors looking to allocate capital across borders. CBDCs can streamline these processes by facilitating direct, peer-to-peer transfers between investors and recipients, reducing the reliance on intermediaries.

The use of CBDCs can significantly speed up the settlement of international investments. Blockchain technology enables real-time or near-real-time transaction processing, eliminating the need for lengthy settlement periods associated with traditional banking systems. This enhanced efficiency can improve liquidity for investors, allowing them to quickly adjust their portfolios in response to market changes.

For instance, an institutional investor looking to invest in a foreign market can use CBDCs to transfer funds directly to the recipient's central bank account. This process can be completed within minutes, compared to the days or even weeks required for traditional wire transfers. The reduced time lag not only enhances the investor's ability to respond to market opportunities but also reduces the risk associated with currency fluctuations during the settlement period.

3.1.2 Reducing Transaction Costs

One of the most significant advantages of CBDCs in the context of cross-border investment flows is the reduction of transaction costs. Traditional international transactions often involve high fees due to the involvement of multiple banks, foreign exchange services, and other intermediaries. These costs can be particularly burdensome for small and medium-sized enterprises (SMEs) and retail investors.

CBDCs can drastically reduce these costs by enabling direct transactions between central banks and financial institutions. The elimination of intermediaries reduces the fees associated with cross-border payments, making it more affordable for investors to move capital across borders. Additionally, the use of smart contracts can automate various aspects of the investment process, further reducing administrative costs and minimizing the risk of errors.

For example, an SME looking to invest in a foreign market can use CBDCs to make a direct investment without incurring high fees for currency conversion and intermediary services. This cost-saving can make international investment more accessible and attractive for smaller businesses, promoting greater global economic integration.

3.1.3 Enhancing Transparency and Security

Transparency and security are critical factors in cross-border investments, where the movement of funds across borders must be carefully monitored to prevent fraud, money laundering, and other illicit activities. Traditional investment processes often lack transparency, making it difficult to trace the flow of funds and ensure compliance with regulatory requirements.

CBDCs can enhance transparency by providing a secure and immutable record of transactions on a blockchain or distributed ledger. Each transaction is recorded in a transparent and tamper-proof manner, allowing regulators, financial institutions, and investors to verify the authenticity and integrity of the transaction. This transparency can help reduce the risk of fraud and ensure that funds are used for their intended purposes.

The security features of blockchain technology can also enhance the safety of cross-border investments. The decentralized nature of blockchain ensures that there is no single point of failure, making it more difficult for malicious actors to compromise the system. Additionally, advanced encryption and authentication measures can protect the digital currency from cyberattacks and data breaches.

For instance, an investor using CBDCs to allocate capital in a foreign market can be confident that their transaction is secure and transparent. The use of blockchain technology ensures that the investment is recorded in an immutable ledger, reducing the risk of fraud and enhancing trust in the transaction.

3.1.4 Facilitating Regulatory Compliance

Regulatory compliance is a critical aspect of cross-border investments, where investors must adhere to various laws and regulations related to anti-money laundering (AML), counter-terrorism financing (CTF), and securities. Ensuring compliance with these regulations can be complex and time-consuming, particularly for investors operating in multiple jurisdictions.

CBDCs can enhance regulatory compliance by providing regulators with greater visibility into cross-border transactions. The transparent and auditable nature of blockchain technology allows regulators to monitor transactions in real-time, identify suspicious activities, and enforce compliance with AML and CTF measures. This increased transparency can help prevent illicit activities and ensure that cross-border investments adhere to regulatory standards.

The programmability of CBDCs can also support automated compliance checks and controls. For example, smart contracts can be designed to automatically flag transactions that exceed certain thresholds or involve high-risk jurisdictions, triggering additional scrutiny or reporting requirements. This automation reduces the administrative burden on investors and ensures that compliance measures are consistently applied.

For example, a multinational corporation using CBDCs to invest in a foreign subsidiary can benefit from automated compliance checks that ensure the transaction adheres to regulatory requirements. The use of smart contracts can streamline the compliance process, reducing the need for manual intervention and minimizing the risk of non-compliance.

3.1.5 Promoting Financial Inclusion

Financial inclusion is another critical benefit of CBDCs in the context of cross-border investments. Traditional financial systems often exclude individuals and businesses in developing countries from accessing global capital markets due to high transaction costs, lack of banking infrastructure, and stringent regulatory requirements. CBDCs can provide a more inclusive financial system by offering secure and efficient payment solutions that do not require traditional banking infrastructure.

By reducing the barriers to entry for cross-border investments, CBDCs can empower individuals and businesses in developing countries to access global capital markets. This can promote economic growth and development by providing new opportunities for investment and trade.

For instance, a small business in a developing country can use CBDCs to attract foreign investment without incurring high fees or navigating complex regulatory requirements. The use of digital currency can provide a secure and transparent means of accessing global capital, enabling the business to expand its operations and contribute to economic growth.

3.1.6 Case Studies: CBDCs in Action

Several countries are exploring the use of CBDCs for cross-border investments through pilot projects and collaborative initiatives. These efforts provide valuable insights into the potential benefits and challenges of implementing CBDCs for international investment flows.

One notable example is Project Jura, a collaboration between the Bank of France and the Swiss National Bank. This project explores the use of CBDCs for cross-border settlements, focusing on improving the efficiency and security of international transactions. The pilot has demonstrated the potential for CBDCs to streamline cross-border investments, reduce transaction costs, and enhance regulatory compliance.

Another example is Project Inthanon-LionRock, a collaboration between the Bank of Thailand and the Hong Kong Monetary Authority. This project aims to develop a cross-border payment system using CBDCs, leveraging blockchain technology to enable real-time, low-cost transactions between participating countries. The pilot has highlighted the importance of interoperability and collaboration between central banks to ensure the seamless integration of different CBDC systems.

The adoption of CBDCs for cross-border investments holds significant promise for transforming the global financial landscape. By providing a more efficient, cost-effective, and transparent solution, CBDCs can enhance the competitiveness of global capital markets, support economic integration, and promote financial inclusion.

However, the successful implementation of CBDCs for cross-border investments requires careful consideration of several factors. Ensuring interoperability between different CBDC systems is crucial to facilitating seamless transactions across borders. Central banks and financial institutions must collaborate to establish common standards and protocols, enabling CBDCs to function harmoniously within the global financial system.

Addressing privacy and security concerns is also critical. While CBDCs can enhance transparency, it is essential to balance this transparency with the need to protect individual privacy and ensure the security of transactions. Robust encryption and authentication measures must be implemented to safeguard against cyberattacks and data breaches.

Regulatory and legal considerations must also be addressed. The incorporation of CBDCs into cross-border investment flows requires clear guidelines and frameworks that define the roles and responsibilities of different stakeholders. Ensuring compliance with AML, CTF, and other regulatory requirements is essential to maintaining the integrity of the global financial system.

3.2 Changing Dynamics in Foreign Direct Investment (FDI)

The advent of Central Bank Digital Currencies (CBDCs) is set to transform the landscape of Foreign Direct Investment (FDI) by altering traditional investment dynamics and introducing new efficiencies, security measures, and opportunities for international investors. This section examines how CBDCs will change the dynamics of FDI, focusing on enhanced efficiency, improved transparency, reduced costs, and greater access for investors.

3.2.1 Streamlining Investment Processes

Foreign Direct Investment typically involves complex processes, including multiple intermediaries, regulatory approvals, and cross-border fund transfers. These steps can lead to delays, increased costs, and complications in managing investments. CBDCs have the potential to streamline these processes by facilitating direct, instant transactions between investors and recipients.

With CBDCs, investors can transfer funds directly to the recipient's account within the central bank's digital currency system, bypassing traditional banking channels. This can significantly reduce the time required for fund transfers, allowing for more agile and responsive investment strategies. The ability to execute transactions in real-time also enhances the liquidity of investments, enabling investors to move funds quickly in response to market conditions.

For example, a multinational corporation looking to invest in a new manufacturing plant abroad can use CBDCs to directly transfer investment capital to the local entity, ensuring faster deployment of funds and more efficient project initiation.

3.2.2 Reducing Transaction and Compliance Costs

One of the primary advantages of CBDCs is the reduction in transaction costs associated with cross-border investments. Traditional FDI processes often involve substantial fees for currency conversion, wire transfers, and intermediary services. These costs can erode the returns on investment and create barriers for smaller investors.

CBDCs eliminate the need for currency conversion and reduce the reliance on intermediaries, leading to lower transaction costs. The use of blockchain technology further enhances efficiency by automating many aspects of the investment process, such as settlement and compliance checks, thereby reducing administrative expenses.

In addition, CBDCs can streamline regulatory compliance by providing a transparent and auditable record of transactions. This can simplify the process of ensuring compliance with anti-money laundering (AML) and counter-terrorism financing (CTF) regulations, reducing the need for costly manual checks and audits. Automated compliance features embedded in smart contracts can further ensure that all regulatory requirements are met efficiently.

For instance, an investor using CBDCs to acquire a stake in a foreign company can benefit from lower transaction fees and streamlined compliance processes, enhancing the overall attractiveness and feasibility of the investment.

3.2.3 Enhancing Transparency and Reducing Risk

Transparency is crucial in FDI, where large sums of money are transferred across borders and the potential for fraud and corruption is high. Traditional investment channels often lack transparency, making it difficult to track funds and ensure they are used appropriately.

CBDCs enhance transparency by recording all transactions on a secure, immutable blockchain ledger. This ensures that every movement of funds can be traced and verified, reducing the risk of fraud and misappropriation. The increased transparency also helps build trust between investors and recipients, fostering a more secure investment environment.

Additionally, the programmable nature of CBDCs allows for the creation of smart contracts that can enforce specific terms and conditions of the investment automatically. This reduces the risk of non-compliance and ensures that funds are released only when predefined criteria are met, such as project milestones or regulatory approvals.

For example, an investment agreement using CBDCs can include smart contracts that automatically disburse funds upon verification of construction progress for an infrastructure project, reducing the risk of delays and misuse of funds.

3.2.4 Facilitating Financial Inclusion and Access

CBDCs have the potential to democratize FDI by lowering entry barriers and providing greater access to global investment opportunities. Traditional FDI channels can be inaccessible to smaller investors and businesses in developing countries due to high costs, complex regulatory requirements, and limited banking infrastructure.

By reducing transaction costs and simplifying compliance processes, CBDCs can make FDI more accessible to a broader range of investors, including small and medium-sized enterprises (SMEs) and individual investors. This can help attract more diverse sources of capital and stimulate economic growth in developing regions.

Furthermore, CBDCs can enhance financial inclusion by providing businesses in emerging markets with access to secure and efficient digital payment solutions. This can enable these businesses to participate more fully in the global economy, attracting foreign investment and fostering economic development.

For instance, a small business in a developing country can use CBDCs to receive investment from foreign investors without the need for costly and complex banking arrangements, facilitating growth and expansion.

3.2.5 Case Studies and Pilot Projects

Several countries are exploring the use of CBDCs to facilitate FDI through pilot projects and collaborative initiatives. These efforts provide valuable insights into the potential benefits and challenges of implementing CBDCs for international investments.

One notable example is Project Helvetia, a collaboration between the Swiss National Bank (SNB) and the Bank for International Settlements (BIS). This project explores the use of wholesale CBDCs for cross-border transactions, focusing on improving the efficiency and security of international investments. The pilot has demonstrated the potential for CBDCs to streamline FDI processes, reduce transaction costs, and enhance regulatory compliance.

Another example is the Digital Dollar Project in the United States, which aims to explore the potential of a US CBDC to enhance the efficiency and transparency of cross-border investments. The project includes pilot programs that assess the impact of CBDCs on international trade and investment, providing valuable insights into best practices and potential pitfalls.

3.2.6 Potential Challenges and Considerations

While the potential benefits of CBDCs for FDI are significant, several challenges and considerations must be addressed to ensure successful implementation. Ensuring interoperability between different CBDC systems is crucial to facilitating seamless cross-border transactions. Central banks and financial institutions must collaborate to establish common standards and protocols, enabling CBDCs to function harmoniously within the global financial system.

Addressing privacy and security concerns is also critical. While CBDCs can enhance transparency, it is essential to balance this transparency with the need to protect individual privacy and ensure the security of transactions. Robust encryption and authentication measures must be implemented to safeguard against cyberattacks and data breaches.

Regulatory and legal considerations must also be addressed. The incorporation of CBDCs into FDI processes requires clear guidelines and frameworks that define the roles and responsibilities of different stakeholders. Ensuring compliance with AML, CTF, and other regulatory requirements is essential to maintaining the integrity of the global financial system.

3.3 CBDCs and the Global Capital Markets

The integration of Central Bank Digital Currencies (CBDCs) into global capital markets is set to reshape the landscape of international finance. CBDCs have the potential to enhance market efficiency, reduce transaction costs, improve liquidity, and provide greater transparency and security. This section explores how CBDCs will impact global capital markets, including their role in trading, investment, and regulatory compliance.

3.3.1 Enhancing Market Efficiency

Global capital markets are vast and complex, involving numerous participants, including investors, issuers, intermediaries, and regulators. Traditional market infrastructures often suffer from inefficiencies due to the involvement of multiple intermediaries, outdated technologies, and fragmented systems. These inefficiencies can lead to delays, increased costs, and reduced liquidity.

CBDCs have the potential to enhance market efficiency by providing a more streamlined and integrated payment and settlement infrastructure. Blockchain technology, which underpins many CBDC initiatives, enables real-time or near-real-time settlement of transactions, eliminating the need for lengthy settlement periods associated with traditional systems. This speed can improve liquidity, allowing market participants to quickly adjust their positions in response to market changes.

For example, in the context of securities trading, the use of CBDCs can enable instant settlement of trades, reducing the time and risk associated with the settlement process. This can enhance the overall efficiency of the market, making it more attractive to investors and issuers.

3.3.2 Reducing Transaction Costs

One of the most significant benefits of CBDCs in global capital markets is the reduction of transaction costs. Traditional financial systems often involve substantial fees for trading, clearing, and settlement due to the involvement of multiple intermediaries. These costs can erode returns on investment and create barriers for smaller market participants.

CBDCs can reduce these costs by facilitating direct transactions between parties, bypassing the need for intermediaries. The use of smart contracts can further enhance efficiency by automating various aspects of the trading and settlement process, reducing administrative expenses and minimizing the risk of errors.

For instance, an investor using CBDCs to purchase shares in a foreign company can benefit from lower transaction fees and faster settlement times, enhancing the overall attractiveness and feasibility of the investment.

3.3.3 Improving Liquidity

Liquidity is a critical factor in global capital markets, where the ability to quickly buy or sell assets without significantly affecting their price is essential. Traditional market infrastructures often suffer from liquidity constraints due to the involvement of multiple intermediaries and the time required for settlement.

CBDCs can improve liquidity by enabling real-time or near-real-time settlement of transactions. This speed ensures that funds are available more quickly, allowing market participants to respond rapidly to market conditions. Enhanced liquidity can reduce price volatility and improve market stability, making capital markets more attractive to investors.

For example, in the context of foreign exchange (FX) markets, the use of CBDCs can enable instant settlement of currency trades, reducing the risk of price fluctuations during the settlement period. This can enhance the efficiency and stability of FX markets, benefiting both investors and issuers.

3.3.4 Enhancing Transparency and Security

Transparency and security are critical factors in global capital markets, where the movement of large sums of money and complex financial instruments must be carefully monitored to prevent fraud, market manipulation, and other illicit activities. Traditional market infrastructures often lack transparency, making it difficult to trace the flow of funds and ensure compliance with regulatory requirements.

CBDCs can enhance transparency by providing a secure and immutable record of transactions on a blockchain or distributed ledger. Each transaction is recorded in a transparent and tamper-proof manner, allowing regulators, financial institutions, and market participants to verify the authenticity and integrity of the transaction. This transparency can help reduce the risk of fraud and market manipulation, enhancing trust and confidence in the market.

The security features of blockchain technology can also enhance the safety of transactions in global capital markets. The decentralized nature of blockchain ensures that there is no single point of failure, making it more difficult for malicious actors to compromise the system. Additionally, advanced encryption and authentication measures can protect the digital currency from cyberattacks and data breaches.

For instance, in the context of bond markets, the use of CBDCs can provide a transparent and secure means of issuing and trading bonds, reducing the risk of fraud and enhancing market integrity.

3.3.5 Facilitating Regulatory Compliance

Regulatory compliance is a critical aspect of global capital markets, where market participants must adhere to various laws and regulations related to anti-money laundering (AML), counter-terrorism financing (CTF), and securities. Ensuring compliance with these regulations can be complex and time-consuming, particularly for participants operating in multiple jurisdictions.

CBDCs can enhance regulatory compliance by providing regulators with greater visibility into market transactions. The transparent and auditable nature of blockchain technology allows regulators to monitor transactions in real-time, identify suspicious activities, and enforce compliance with AML and CTF measures. This increased transparency can help prevent illicit activities and ensure that market participants adhere to regulatory standards.

The programmability of CBDCs can also support automated compliance checks and controls. For example, smart contracts can be designed to automatically flag transactions that exceed certain thresholds or involve high-risk jurisdictions, triggering additional scrutiny or reporting requirements. This automation reduces the administrative burden on market participants and ensures that compliance measures are consistently applied.

For instance, a financial institution using CBDCs to trade

securities can benefit from automated compliance checks that ensure the transaction adheres to regulatory requirements. The use of smart contracts can streamline the compliance process, reducing the need for manual intervention and minimizing the risk of non-compliance.

3.3.6 Case Studies and Pilot Projects

Several countries and financial institutions are exploring the use of CBDCs in global capital markets through pilot projects and collaborative initiatives. These efforts provide valuable insights into the potential benefits and challenges of implementing CBDCs for trading, investment, and regulatory compliance.

One notable example is Project Helvetia, a collaboration between the Swiss National Bank (SNB) and the Bank for International Settlements (BIS). This project explores the use of wholesale CBDCs for cross-border transactions, focusing on improving the efficiency and security of international investments. The pilot has demonstrated the potential for CBDCs to streamline trading and settlement processes, reduce transaction costs, and enhance regulatory compliance.

Another example is Project Ubin, a collaboration between the Monetary Authority of Singapore (MAS) and several financial institutions. This project explores the use of blockchain and distributed ledger technology (DLT) for interbank payments and settlements, focusing on enhancing market efficiency and reducing risks. The pilot has highlighted the importance of interoperability and collaboration between central banks to ensure the seamless integration of different CBDC systems.

The adoption of CBDCs in global capital markets holds significant promise for transforming the landscape of international finance. By providing a more efficient, cost-effective, and transparent solution, CBDCs can enhance market efficiency, improve liquidity, and promote regulatory compliance.

However, the successful implementation of CBDCs in global capital markets requires careful consideration of several factors. Ensuring interoperability between different CBDC systems is crucial to facilitating seamless transactions across borders. Central banks and financial institutions must collaborate to establish common standards and protocols, enabling CBDCs to function harmoniously within the global financial system.

Addressing privacy and security concerns is also critical. While CBDCs can enhance transparency, it is essential to balance this transparency with the need to protect individual privacy and ensure the security of transactions. Robust encryption and authentication measures must be implemented to safeguard against cyberattacks and data breaches.

Regulatory and legal considerations must also be addressed. The incorporation of CBDCs into global capital markets requires clear guidelines and frameworks that define the roles and responsibilities of different stakeholders. Ensuring compliance with AML, CTF, and other regulatory requirements is essential to maintaining the integrity of the global financial system.

3.4 Case Studies: Investment Trends in CBDC

As Central Bank Digital Currencies (CBDCs) gain traction globally, their impact on investment trends is becoming increasingly evident. This section examines various case studies from early adopters and pilot projects, highlighting how CBDCs are influencing investment behaviors, shaping market dynamics, and offering new opportunities and challenges for investors.

3.4.1 The Digital Yuan: Catalyzing Investment in China

China's Digital Currency Electronic Payment (DCEP), commonly known as the digital yuan, represents one of the most advanced

CBDC initiatives globally. The People's Bank of China (PBOC) has been at the forefront of this development, aiming to modernize the country's financial system, enhance monetary policy control, and reduce reliance on the US dollar in international trade and finance.

The introduction of the digital yuan has had a significant impact on investment trends within China. One notable effect is the increased efficiency in cross-border investments. By reducing the time and cost associated with traditional cross-border transactions, the digital yuan has made it easier for foreign investors to participate in the Chinese market. This increased accessibility has attracted more foreign direct investment (FDI) into China, particularly in sectors such as technology, manufacturing, and infrastructure.

Moreover, the transparency and security provided by the digital yuan have increased investor confidence. Blockchain technology ensures that all transactions are recorded in an immutable ledger, reducing the risk of fraud and enhancing trust in the financial system. This transparency has made China a more attractive destination for international investors seeking secure and efficient investment opportunities.

3.4.2 The Sand Dollar: Boosting Local and Foreign Investments in The Bahamas

The Sand Dollar, launched by the Central Bank of The Bahamas in October 2020, is one of the first fully operational retail CBDCs in the world. The primary goal of the Sand Dollar is to enhance financial inclusion, improve payment efficiency, and support economic development in the archipelago.

The introduction of the Sand Dollar has positively impacted both local and foreign investments in The Bahamas. For local businesses, the Sand Dollar provides a secure and efficient means of receiving and making payments, reducing the reliance on cash and traditional banking infrastructure. This increased efficiency has enabled local businesses to attract more investments, both domestically and from abroad.

Foreign investors have also benefited from the Sand Dollar's transparency and reduced transaction costs. The ability to conduct transactions in real-time without the need for multiple intermediaries has made The Bahamas a more attractive destination for investment. This has been particularly beneficial for sectors such as tourism, real estate, and financial services, where the speed and security of transactions are critical.

The Central Bank of The Bahamas has also leveraged the Sand Dollar to promote sustainable investment practices. By providing a transparent and auditable record of transactions, the Sand Dollar has enabled better tracking of investments in sustainable and green projects. This has attracted environmentally conscious investors looking to support sustainable development in the region.

3.4.3 The e-Krona: Facilitating Investments in Sweden

Sweden's e-Krona project, initiated by the Riksbank, aims to provide a digital complement to cash, ensuring that the public continues to have access to central bank money in a digital age. The e-Krona project has significant implications for investment trends within Sweden, particularly in the context of financial inclusion and market efficiency.

The introduction of the e-Krona has made it easier for individuals and businesses to access financial services, promoting greater financial inclusion. This increased access has facilitated more investments in local businesses, particularly small and medium-sized enterprises (SMEs) that may have previously faced barriers to accessing capital.

For international investors, the e-Krona offers a secure and efficient means of investing in the Swedish market. The transparency and security provided by blockchain technology have increased investor confidence, making Sweden a more attractive destination for foreign investments. The ability to conduct transactions in real-time has also improved liquidity in the market, enabling investors to respond more quickly to market opportunities.

One notable impact of the e-Krona project has been the increased investment in Sweden's technology sector. The country's robust digital infrastructure and supportive regulatory environment have made it a hub for tech startups and innovation. The e-Krona has further enhanced this attractiveness by providing a secure and efficient means of conducting transactions and raising capital.

3.4.4 Project Ubin: Transforming Investments in Singapore

Project Ubin, led by the Monetary Authority of Singapore (MAS), explores the use of blockchain and distributed ledger technology (DLT) for wholesale CBDCs. The project aims to improve the efficiency, security, and transparency of Singapore's financial infrastructure, with significant implications for investment trends in the region.

The implementation of Project Ubin has enhanced the efficiency of interbank payments and settlements, reducing the time and costs associated with traditional systems. This increased efficiency has made Singapore a more attractive destination for international investments, particularly in sectors such as finance, technology, and real estate.

The transparency provided by blockchain technology has also increased investor confidence in the Singaporean market. By providing a secure and immutable record of transactions, Project Ubin has reduced the risk of fraud and market manipulation, enhancing trust in the financial system. This transparency has attracted more foreign investments, supporting Singapore's position as a global financial hub.

One notable impact of Project Ubin has been the increased investment in Singapore's fintech sector. The country's supportive regulatory environment and advanced digital infrastructure have made it a hub for fintech innovation. Project Ubin has further enhanced this attractiveness by providing a secure and efficient means of conducting transactions and raising capital.

3.4.5 The Digital Euro: Shaping Investments in the Eurozone

The European Central Bank (ECB) has been actively exploring the development of a digital euro, reflecting the growing interest in CBDCs among advanced economies. The digital euro project aims to complement the existing euro currency, providing a digital alternative that enhances payment efficiency and supports financial stability.

The introduction of the digital euro has significant implications for investment trends within the eurozone. One notable effect is the increased efficiency in cross-border investments. By reducing the time and cost associated with traditional cross-border transactions, the digital euro has made it easier for investors to participate in markets across the eurozone. This increased accessibility has attracted more foreign direct investment (FDI) into the region, particularly in sectors such as technology, manufacturing, and infrastructure.

The transparency and security provided by the digital euro have also increased investor confidence. Blockchain technology ensures that all transactions are recorded in an immutable ledger, reducing the risk of fraud and enhancing trust in the financial system. This transparency has made the eurozone a more attractive destination for international investors seeking secure and efficient investment opportunities.

3.4.6 The Digital Dollar Project: Transforming Investments in the United States

The Digital Dollar Project is a collaboration between the Digital Dollar Foundation and Accenture, aiming to explore the potential benefits and challenges of a US CBDC. The project includes pilot programs to assess the impact of CBDCs on international trade and investment, providing valuable insights into best practices and potential pitfalls.

The introduction of a digital dollar has significant implications for investment trends in the United States. One notable effect is the increased efficiency in cross-border investments. By reducing the time and cost associated with traditional cross-border transactions, the digital dollar has made it easier for foreign investors to participate in the US market. This increased accessibility has attracted more foreign direct investment (FDI) into the country, particularly in sectors such as technology, manufacturing, and infrastructure.

The transparency and security provided by the digital dollar have also increased investor confidence. Blockchain technology ensures that all transactions are recorded in an immutable ledger, reducing the risk of fraud and enhancing trust in the financial system. This transparency has made the United States a more attractive destination for international investors seeking secure and efficient investment opportunities.

3.4.7 Cross-Border Initiatives: The m-CBDC Bridge Project

The m-CBDC Bridge Project is a collaborative initiative involving multiple central banks, including the Hong Kong Monetary Authority, the Bank of Thailand, the Central Bank of the United Arab Emirates, and the People's Bank of China. This project aims to develop a cross-border payment system using multiple CBDCs, leveraging blockchain technology to enable real-time, low-cost transactions between participating countries.

The m-CBDC Bridge Project has demonstrated the feasibility of using CBDCs to facilitate cross-border investments, significantly reducing transaction times and costs compared to traditional methods. The pilot has also highlighted the importance of interoperability and collaboration between central banks to ensure the seamless integration of different CBDC systems.

The success of the m-CBDC Bridge Project has provided valuable insights into the potential for CBDCs to enhance international trade and investment flows. By providing a secure and efficient payment infrastructure, the project has shown how digital currencies can support the objectives of international trade agreements and promote economic integration.

These case studies highlight the diverse approaches and motivations behind the development and implementation of CBDCs across global markets. From enhancing payment efficiency and reducing transaction costs to supporting financial inclusion and regulatory compliance, CBDCs offer a wide range of benefits for both domestic and international investments.

The lessons learned from these early adopters and pilot projects provide valuable insights into the potential of CBDCs to transform global investment trends. As more countries explore and implement digital currencies, continued innovation and collaboration will be essential to realizing the full potential of CBDCs in enhancing global trade and investment. The future of global capital markets looks increasingly digital, with CBDCs playing a pivotal role in shaping the next generation of international finance.

CHAPTER 4: REDEFINING TRADE FINANCING

4.1 CBDCs and the Transformation of Trade Finance

Trade finance, the backbone of international trade, involves various financial instruments and products that facilitate global commerce by providing financing and mitigating risks associated with international transactions. Central Bank Digital Currencies (CBDCs) offer significant potential to transform trade finance by enhancing efficiency, reducing costs, and improving transparency and security. This section explores how CBDCs can redefine trade finance, examining their impact on key aspects such as letters of credit, supply chain finance, and risk management.

4.1.1 The Role of Trade Finance

Trade finance encompasses a wide range of financial instruments and services designed to support international trade. Key instruments include letters of credit (LCs), trade credit, and supply chain finance. These tools help manage the financial risks associated with cross-border transactions, providing assurance to both buyers and sellers that their interests are protected.

Traditional trade finance processes are often complex and involve multiple intermediaries, including banks, insurers, and logistics providers. These processes can be time-consuming and costly, leading to inefficiencies and delays in the movement of goods and payments.

4.1.2 Enhancing Efficiency with CBDCs

CBDCs have the potential to streamline trade finance processes by providing a more efficient and transparent payment and settlement infrastructure. Blockchain technology, which underpins many CBDC initiatives, enables real-time or near-real-time settlement of transactions, reducing the time and cost associated with traditional systems.

For instance, the use of CBDCs can significantly improve the efficiency of letters of credit. Traditionally, LCs involve a series of checks and verifications by banks and other intermediaries, leading to delays and increased costs. With CBDCs, the process can be automated using smart contracts. These self-executing contracts can automatically verify the terms of the LC and release payment once the conditions are met, such as the delivery of goods and submission of shipping documents.

An example of this can be seen in the potential transformation of an international trade transaction. A buyer in one country can issue an LC backed by CBDCs. Once the seller ships the goods and the shipping documents are verified, the smart contract can automatically release the payment from the buyer's CBDC account to the seller's account, completing the transaction in a fraction of the time required by traditional methods.

4.1.3 Reducing Costs

One of the most significant benefits of CBDCs in trade finance is the reduction of transaction costs. Traditional trade finance processes often involve high fees due to the participation of multiple intermediaries, currency conversion costs, and the complexity of verifying documents and compliance with regulations.

CBDCs can reduce these costs by facilitating direct transactions between parties, eliminating the need for intermediaries. The use of blockchain technology further enhances efficiency by automating many aspects of the trade finance process, reducing administrative expenses and minimizing the risk of errors.

For example, in supply chain finance, suppliers often face delays in receiving payments for goods shipped to buyers. With CBDCs, payments can be made instantly upon verification of delivery, reducing the need for costly short-term financing solutions such as factoring. This can lower the overall cost of financing for suppliers and improve their cash flow management.

4.1.4 Improving Transparency and Security

Transparency and security are critical factors in trade finance, where the movement of goods and funds across borders must be carefully monitored to prevent fraud and ensure compliance with regulations. Traditional trade finance processes often lack transparency, making it difficult to trace the flow of funds and verify the authenticity of transactions.

CBDCs can enhance transparency by providing a secure and immutable record of transactions on a blockchain or distributed ledger. Each transaction is recorded in a transparent and tamper-proof manner, allowing all parties involved to verify the authenticity and integrity of the transaction. This transparency can help reduce the risk of fraud and ensure that funds are used for their intended purposes.

For instance, in a trade finance transaction using CBDCs, the movement of funds can be tracked from the buyer to the seller, with each step recorded on the blockchain. This provides a clear audit trail that can be accessed by regulators, auditors, and other stakeholders, enhancing trust and confidence in the transaction.

The security features of blockchain technology also enhance the safety of trade finance transactions. The decentralized nature of blockchain ensures that there is no single point of failure, making it more difficult for malicious actors to compromise the system. Additionally, advanced encryption and authentication measures can protect the digital currency from cyberattacks and data breaches.

4.1.5 Facilitating Supply Chain Finance

Supply chain finance involves providing financing to suppliers based on the value of their receivables. This form of financing helps suppliers improve their cash flow by receiving payments earlier than the agreed payment terms. Traditional supply chain finance processes can be complex and costly, involving multiple intermediaries and manual verification of documents.

CBDCs can streamline supply chain finance by providing a secure and efficient means of transferring funds directly between buyers and suppliers. The use of smart contracts can automate the process of verifying delivery and releasing payment, reducing the time and cost associated with traditional methods.

For example, a buyer can use CBDCs to issue a payment commitment to a supplier upon receiving goods. The payment can be automatically released once the delivery is confirmed and verified through the blockchain. This not only speeds up the payment process but also reduces the risk of disputes and fraud.

4.1.6 Case Studies: CBDCs in Trade Finance

Several countries and financial institutions are exploring the use of CBDCs in trade finance through pilot projects and collaborative initiatives. These efforts provide valuable insights into the potential benefits and challenges of implementing CBDCs in trade finance.

One notable example is the collaboration between the Hong Kong Monetary Authority (HKMA) and the Bank of Thailand. Their joint initiative, Project Inthanon-LionRock, explores the use of CBDCs for cross-border trade finance, leveraging blockchain technology to enable real-time, low-cost transactions. The pilot has demonstrated the feasibility of using CBDCs to streamline trade finance processes, reduce transaction costs, and enhance transparency and security.

Another example is the Digital Trade Chain (DTC) consortium, a collaboration between several European banks. The consortium is developing a blockchain-based platform to facilitate trade finance for SMEs. By using CBDCs and smart contracts, the platform aims to automate trade finance processes, reduce costs, and improve access to financing for small businesses.

The adoption of CBDCs in trade finance holds significant promise for transforming the landscape of international commerce. By providing a more efficient, cost-effective, and transparent solution, CBDCs can enhance the competitiveness of businesses, support economic integration, and promote financial inclusion.

However, the successful implementation of CBDCs in trade finance requires careful consideration of several factors. Ensuring interoperability between different CBDC systems is crucial to facilitating seamless transactions across borders. Central banks and financial institutions must collaborate to establish common standards and protocols, enabling CBDCs to function harmoniously within the global financial system.

Addressing privacy and security concerns is also critical. While CBDCs can enhance transparency, it is essential to balance this transparency with the need to protect individual privacy and ensure the security of transactions. Robust encryption and authentication measures must be implemented to safeguard against cyberattacks and data breaches.

Regulatory and legal considerations must also be addressed. The incorporation of CBDCs into trade finance processes requires clear guidelines and frameworks that define the roles and responsibilities of different stakeholders. Ensuring compliance with AML, CTF, and other regulatory requirements is essential to maintaining the integrity of the global financial system.

4.2 Digital Letters of Credit and Smart Contracts

The integration of Central Bank Digital Currencies (CBDCs) with digital letters of credit and smart contracts represents a significant advancement in trade finance. These technologies promise to enhance the efficiency, security, and transparency of trade transactions. This section explores the transformation of letters of credit through digitalization and the role of smart contracts in automating and securing trade finance processes.

4.2.1 Traditional Letters of Credit: Challenges and Limitations

Letters of credit (LCs) are a cornerstone of international trade, providing a secure payment mechanism that mitigates the risks associated with cross-border transactions. In a traditional LC arrangement, a buyer's bank guarantees payment to the seller upon the presentation of specified documents, such as shipping and insurance certificates, that confirm the shipment of goods.

While LCs offer significant security and trust, they also come with several challenges and limitations:

- Complexity and Manual Processes: Traditional LCs involve complex and labor-intensive processes, including document verification, manual handling, and coordination between multiple parties (buyers, sellers, banks, and shipping companies). These processes are time-consuming and prone to errors.
- High Costs: The involvement of multiple intermediaries and

the extensive documentation required for LCs result in high transaction costs. These costs can be particularly burdensome for small and medium-sized enterprises (SMEs).

- Delays: The manual verification of documents and the need for physical paper trails can cause significant delays in the completion of trade transactions, affecting cash flow and the timely delivery of goods.

- Fraud Risk: The reliance on physical documents and manual processes increases the risk of document fraud and forgery, potentially leading to disputes and financial losses.

4.2.2 Digital Letters of Credit: Streamlining Trade Transactions

The digitalization of letters of credit addresses many of the challenges associated with traditional LCs by leveraging blockchain technology and smart contracts. Digital LCs offer a more efficient, secure, and transparent solution for trade finance.

- Efficiency and Speed: Digital LCs streamline the process by digitizing the documentation and verification processes. Blockchain technology enables real-time sharing and verification of documents, significantly reducing the time required to complete trade transactions. This efficiency is particularly beneficial for industries where timely delivery of goods is critical.

- Cost Reduction: By eliminating the need for physical documents and reducing the reliance on intermediaries, digital LCs can lower transaction costs. The automation of document verification through smart contracts further reduces administrative expenses and minimizes the risk of errors.

- Enhanced Security: Blockchain technology provides a secure and immutable record of transactions. Each step in the LC process is recorded on the blockchain, ensuring transparency and traceability. This reduces the risk of fraud and enhances trust between trading partners.

- Transparency: Digital LCs offer greater transparency by

providing all parties involved with real-time access to transaction data and document status. This visibility helps prevent disputes and ensures that all conditions of the LC are met before payment is released.

4.2.3 The Role of Smart Contracts in Digital LCs

Smart contracts are self-executing contracts with the terms of the agreement directly written into code. They automatically enforce and execute the terms of the contract when predefined conditions are met. In the context of digital letters of credit, smart contracts play a crucial role in automating and securing trade transactions.

- Automation of Processes: Smart contracts automate the verification and approval processes involved in LCs. For example, a smart contract can be programmed to automatically release payment to the seller once the shipping documents are uploaded and verified on the blockchain. This automation reduces the need for manual intervention and speeds up the transaction process.
- Conditional Payments: Smart contracts ensure that payments are made only when specific conditions are met. For instance, payment can be triggered upon the confirmation of delivery, inspection of goods, or compliance with regulatory requirements. This conditionality provides assurance to both buyers and sellers that the terms of the trade agreement will be honored.
- Immutable Records: The use of blockchain and smart contracts ensures that all transaction data and document records are immutable and tamper-proof. This immutability enhances the integrity of the LC process and provides a clear audit trail for regulators and auditors.

4.2.4 Case Studies: Digital LCs and Smart Contracts in Action

Several pilot projects and initiatives are exploring the use of digital LCs and smart contracts to enhance trade finance processes. These case studies provide valuable insights into the practical applications and benefits of these technologies.

- TradeLens: TradeLens is a blockchain-based platform developed by Maersk and IBM that aims to digitize the global supply chain and improve the efficiency of trade finance. The platform uses smart contracts to automate the documentation and verification processes involved in LCs. By providing real-time visibility and transparency, TradeLens reduces delays and costs associated with traditional LCs.

- Marco Polo Network: The Marco Polo Network is a blockchain-based trade finance platform that leverages digital LCs and smart contracts to streamline trade transactions. The platform enables real-time sharing and verification of trade documents, reducing the time and cost required for cross-border transactions. By automating the LC process, the Marco Polo Network enhances security and transparency in trade finance.

- Voltron: Voltron is a blockchain-based trade finance platform developed by a consortium of banks, including HSBC and Standard Chartered. The platform uses smart contracts to automate the issuance and verification of digital LCs. By providing a secure and transparent environment for trade transactions, Voltron reduces the risk of fraud and enhances trust between trading partners.

The integration of CBDCs with digital letters of credit and smart contracts holds significant promise for transforming trade finance. By providing a more efficient, secure, and transparent solution, these technologies can enhance the competitiveness of businesses, support economic integration, and promote financial inclusion.

However, several challenges and considerations must be addressed to ensure successful implementation:

- Interoperability: Ensuring interoperability between different blockchain platforms and CBDC systems is crucial for facilitating seamless cross-border transactions. Standardization of protocols and collaboration between central banks and financial institutions are essential to achieving this interoperability.

- Regulatory Compliance: Clear guidelines and frameworks are needed to define the roles and responsibilities of different stakeholders in the digital LC process. Ensuring compliance with AML, CTF, and other regulatory requirements is essential to maintaining the integrity of the global financial system.

- Privacy and Security: While digital LCs and smart contracts enhance transparency, it is essential to balance this transparency with the need to protect individual privacy and ensure the security of transactions. Robust encryption and authentication measures must be implemented to safeguard against cyberattacks and data breaches.

As more countries and financial institutions explore and implement digital LCs and smart contracts, the lessons learned from pilot projects and early adopters will provide valuable insights into best practices and potential pitfalls. Continued innovation and collaboration will be key to realizing the full potential of CBDCs in transforming trade finance and fostering a more inclusive and efficient global economy.

4.3 Risk Management in Trade Financing with CBDCs

Risk management is a crucial aspect of trade finance, where various types of risks such as credit risk, operational risk, and fraud can significantly impact the financial health of businesses involved in international trade. Central Bank Digital Currencies (CBDCs) offer a transformative solution to enhance risk management in trade financing by leveraging the inherent features of blockchain technology and smart contracts. This section explores how CBDCs can mitigate different types of risks in trade finance, providing a more secure and efficient framework for global commerce.

4.3.1 Mitigating Credit Risk

Credit risk, the risk that a counterparty will default on its contractual obligations, is a significant concern in trade finance. Traditional trade finance instruments like letters of credit (LCs) and trade credit insurance are designed to mitigate this risk, but they often involve complex and costly processes.

CBDCs can enhance credit risk management by providing a transparent and immutable record of transactions on a blockchain. This transparency allows all parties involved to verify the authenticity and integrity of transactions, reducing the risk of default and disputes. Additionally, the use of smart contracts can automate the enforcement of contractual terms, ensuring that payments are made only when predefined conditions are met.

For example, in a trade transaction using a CBDC-based LC, the buyer's payment obligation can be automatically fulfilled once the seller provides proof of shipment and delivery. The smart contract ensures that payment is released only when the conditions specified in the LC are met, reducing the risk of default and increasing trust between trading partners.

4.3.2 Reducing Operational Risk

Operational risk in trade finance arises from inefficiencies and errors in the execution of trade transactions. Traditional trade finance processes often involve manual handling of documents, multiple intermediaries, and complex verification procedures, increasing the likelihood of errors and delays.

CBDCs can significantly reduce operational risk by automating and streamlining trade finance processes. The use of blockchain technology ensures that all transaction data is recorded in a secure and tamper-proof ledger, reducing the risk of errors and inconsistencies. Smart contracts further enhance efficiency by automating the verification and execution of trade transactions, minimizing the need for manual intervention.

For instance, a trade finance transaction using CBDCs can involve the automated verification of shipping documents and the release of payment upon confirmation of delivery. This automation reduces the risk of human error and ensures that the transaction is executed accurately and efficiently.

4.3.3 Enhancing Fraud Prevention

Fraud is a significant risk in trade finance, where the manipulation of documents and misrepresentation of goods can lead to substantial financial losses. Traditional trade finance processes, which rely heavily on physical documents and manual verification, are particularly vulnerable to fraud.

CBDCs can enhance fraud prevention by providing a secure and transparent record of all trade transactions. Blockchain technology ensures that each transaction is recorded in an immutable ledger, making it difficult for malicious actors to alter or manipulate transaction data. The use of smart contracts further enhances security by automating the verification and execution of transactions based on predefined conditions.

For example, in a trade finance transaction using CBDCs, the authenticity of shipping documents can be verified through blockchain technology, ensuring that only genuine documents are accepted. Smart contracts can automatically execute the transaction once the conditions specified in the trade agreement are met, reducing the risk of fraud and enhancing trust between trading partners.

4.3.4 Facilitating Regulatory Compliance

Regulatory compliance is a critical aspect of trade finance, where businesses must adhere to various laws and regulations related to anti-money laundering (AML), counter-terrorism financing (CTF), and trade sanctions. Ensuring compliance with these regulations can be complex and time-consuming, particularly for businesses operating in multiple jurisdictions.

CBDCs can facilitate regulatory compliance by providing regulators with greater visibility into trade transactions. The transparent and auditable nature of blockchain technology allows regulators to monitor transactions in real-time, identify suspicious activities, and enforce compliance with AML and CTF measures. This increased transparency helps prevent illicit activities and ensures that trade transactions adhere to regulatory standards.

Additionally, the programmability of CBDCs allows for the implementation of automated compliance checks and controls. Smart contracts can be designed to automatically flag transactions that exceed certain thresholds or involve high-risk jurisdictions, triggering additional scrutiny or reporting requirements. This automation reduces the administrative burden on businesses and ensures that compliance measures are consistently applied.

For example, a financial institution using CBDCs for trade finance can benefit from automated compliance checks that ensure each transaction adheres to AML and CTF regulations. Smart contracts can automatically verify the identity of parties involved and flag any suspicious transactions for further investigation, reducing the risk of regulatory non-compliance.

4.3.5 Case Studies: Risk Management with CBDCs in Trade Finance

Several pilot projects and initiatives are exploring the use of CBDCs to enhance risk management in trade finance. These case studies provide valuable insights into the practical applications and benefits of CBDCs in mitigating various types of risks.

- Project Jasper-Ubin: A collaborative initiative between the Bank of Canada and the Monetary Authority of Singapore, Project Jasper-Ubin explores the use of blockchain and distributed ledger technology (DLT) for cross-border payments and settlements. The project demonstrated the potential of CBDCs to reduce operational risk by automating the verification and settlement of transactions, enhancing transparency, and reducing the risk of fraud.

- We.Trade: We.Trade is a blockchain-based trade finance platform developed by a consortium of European banks. The platform uses smart contracts to automate trade finance processes, reducing operational risk and enhancing fraud prevention. By providing a secure and transparent environment for trade transactions, We.Trade has demonstrated the potential of CBDCs to enhance risk management in trade finance.

- Marco Polo Network: The Marco Polo Network is a blockchain-based trade finance platform that leverages CBDCs and smart contracts to streamline trade transactions. The platform enhances risk management by providing a secure and transparent record of transactions, reducing the risk of fraud and ensuring compliance with regulatory requirements.

The adoption of CBDCs in trade finance holds significant promise for enhancing risk management and transforming the landscape of international commerce. By providing a more efficient, secure, and transparent solution, CBDCs can mitigate various types of risks and enhance the competitiveness of businesses engaged in global trade.

However, several challenges and considerations must be addressed to ensure successful implementation:

- Interoperability: Ensuring interoperability between different CBDC systems and blockchain platforms is crucial for facilitating seamless cross-border transactions. Standardization of protocols and collaboration between central banks and financial institutions are essential to achieving this interoperability.

- Regulatory Frameworks: Clear guidelines and frameworks are needed to define the roles and responsibilities of different stakeholders in the CBDC-based trade finance process. Ensuring compliance with AML, CTF, and other regulatory requirements is essential to maintaining the integrity of the global financial system.

- Privacy and Security: While CBDCs enhance transparency, it is essential to balance this transparency with the need to protect individual privacy and ensure the security of transactions. Robust encryption and authentication measures must be implemented to safeguard against cyberattacks and data breaches.

As more countries and financial institutions explore and implement CBDCs for trade finance, the lessons learned from pilot projects and early adopters will provide valuable insights into best practices and potential pitfalls. Continued innovation and collaboration will be key to realizing the full potential of CBDCs in enhancing risk management and fostering a more inclusive and efficient global economy.

4.4 Case Studies: Enhanced Trade Financing Mechanisms

The advent of Central Bank Digital Currencies (CBDCs) is revolutionizing trade finance by introducing more efficient, secure, and transparent mechanisms. Various pilot projects and initiatives across the globe demonstrate how CBDCs can enhance trade finance, offering valuable insights into their practical applications and benefits. This section delves into specific case studies that highlight the transformative impact of CBDCs on trade finance.

4.4.1 PROJECT INTHANON-LIONROCK: CROSS-BORDER PAYMENTS BETWEEN THAILAND AND HONG KONG

Project Inthanon-LionRock is a collaborative initiative between the Hong Kong Monetary Authority (HKMA) and the Bank of Thailand (BOT), aimed at exploring the potential of CBDCs for cross-border payments and trade finance. This project leverages blockchain technology to enhance the efficiency, security, and transparency of trade transactions between Thailand and Hong Kong.

Key Features and Achievements:

- Real-Time Settlement: The project demonstrated the capability of CBDCs to facilitate real-time settlement of cross-border transactions, significantly reducing the time required for payment processing. This real-time settlement enhances liquidity for businesses and reduces the risk associated with delayed payments.

- Cost Reduction: By eliminating intermediaries and reducing the need for multiple currency conversions, Project Inthanon-LionRock achieved substantial cost savings. Businesses engaged in cross-border trade benefited from lower transaction fees and more competitive pricing.

- Enhanced Transparency and Security: The use of blockchain technology ensured that all transactions were recorded in a secure, tamper-proof ledger. This transparency reduced the risk of fraud and increased trust between trading partners.

Impact on Trade Finance:

Project Inthanon-LionRock highlighted the potential of CBDCs to streamline trade finance processes, making them more efficient and cost-effective. The success of this project demonstrated that CBDCs could provide a robust framework for cross-border trade, fostering greater economic integration between participating countries.

4.4.2 THE MARCO POLO NETWORK: STREAMLINING TRADE FINANCE WITH BLOCKCHAIN AND CBDCS

The Marco Polo Network is a blockchain-based trade finance platform that leverages CBDCs and smart contracts to automate and secure trade transactions. Developed by a consortium of banks, including BNP Paribas, ING, and Commerzbank, the Marco Polo Network aims to enhance trade finance by providing a seamless and transparent digital infrastructure.

Key Features and Achievements:

- Automated Trade Processes: The platform uses smart contracts to automate various aspects of trade finance, including the issuance of letters of credit, verification of shipping documents, and release of payments. This automation reduces the need for manual intervention, minimizing errors and delays.

- Interoperability: The Marco Polo Network ensures interoperability with existing financial systems, allowing seamless integration with traditional banking infrastructure. This interoperability enhances the usability of the platform and encourages wider adoption.

- Fraud Prevention: By recording all transactions on a blockchain, the platform provides a transparent and immutable record of trade activities. This transparency reduces the risk of fraud and increases trust between trading partners.

Impact on Trade Finance:

The Marco Polo Network has demonstrated the potential of CBDCs and blockchain technology to transform trade finance by enhancing efficiency, reducing costs, and improving security. The platform's success underscores the importance of collaboration between financial institutions and technology providers in developing innovative trade finance solutions.

4.4.3 TRADELENS: DIGITIZING GLOBAL TRADE WITH BLOCKCHAIN AND CBDCS

TradeLens is a blockchain-based platform developed by Maersk and IBM to digitize global trade and improve the efficiency of trade finance. The platform leverages CBDCs and smart contracts to automate trade processes, enhance transparency, and reduce costs.

Key Features and Achievements:

- Real-Time Visibility: TradeLens provides real-time visibility into the status of shipments and trade documents, enabling all parties involved to track and verify transactions seamlessly. This visibility reduces delays and improves coordination between trading partners.

- Automated Document Management: The platform uses smart contracts to automate the verification and approval of trade documents, reducing the need for manual processing. This automation enhances efficiency and reduces the risk of errors.

- Enhanced Security: By recording all transactions on a secure blockchain, TradeLens ensures the integrity and authenticity of trade data. This security reduces the risk of fraud and increases trust between trading partners.

Impact on Trade Finance:

TradeLens has demonstrated the potential of CBDCs and blockchain technology to revolutionize trade finance by providing a more efficient, transparent, and secure framework for global trade. The platform's success highlights the importance of digital transformation in enhancing trade finance processes and supporting economic growth.

4.4.4 WE.TRADE: FACILITATING SME TRADE FINANCE WITH BLOCKCHAIN AND CBDCS

We.Trade is a blockchain-based trade finance platform developed by a consortium of European banks, including HSBC, UniCredit, and Deutsche Bank. The platform aims to simplify and enhance trade finance for small and medium-sized enterprises (SMEs) by leveraging CBDCs and smart contracts.

Key Features and Achievements:

- Simplified Trade Processes: We.Trade simplifies trade finance processes by providing a digital platform for issuing letters of credit, verifying trade documents, and releasing payments. This simplification reduces the administrative burden on SMEs and enhances efficiency.

- Transparency and Trust: By recording all transactions on a blockchain, We.Trade provides a transparent and immutable record of trade activities. This transparency reduces the risk of fraud and increases trust between trading partners.

- Cost-Effective Solutions: The platform offers cost-effective trade finance solutions for SMEs, reducing the high fees associated with traditional trade finance instruments. This cost reduction makes trade finance more accessible for smaller businesses.

Impact on Trade Finance:

We.Trade has demonstrated the potential of CBDCs and blockchain technology to enhance trade finance for SMEs by providing a simplified, transparent, and cost-effective solution. The platform's success underscores the importance of innovation in supporting the growth and competitiveness of SMEs in the global market.

4.4.5 PROJECT HELVETIA: EXPLORING WHOLESALE CBDCS FOR TRADE FINANCE

Project Helvetia is a collaborative initiative between the Swiss National Bank (SNB) and the Bank for International Settlements (BIS) that explores the use of wholesale CBDCs for trade finance. The project aims to enhance the efficiency and security of cross-border trade transactions by leveraging blockchain technology and CBDCs.

Key Features and Achievements:

- Real-Time Settlement: Project Helvetia demonstrated the capability of wholesale CBDCs to facilitate real-time settlement of trade transactions, reducing the time required for payment processing and enhancing liquidity for businesses.

- Cost Reduction: By eliminating intermediaries and reducing the need for multiple currency conversions, the project achieved substantial cost savings for businesses engaged in cross-border trade.

- Enhanced Security and Compliance: The use of blockchain technology ensured that all transactions were recorded in a secure, tamper-proof ledger, enhancing transparency and compliance with regulatory requirements.

Impact on Trade Finance:

Project Helvetia highlighted the potential of wholesale CBDCs to transform trade finance by providing a more efficient, secure, and transparent framework for cross-border transactions. The project's success demonstrated the importance of collaboration between central banks and financial institutions in developing innovative trade finance solutions.

The adoption of CBDCs in trade finance holds significant promise for enhancing the efficiency, security, and transparency of global trade. As more countries and financial institutions explore and implement CBDCs, the lessons learned from pilot projects and early adopters will provide valuable insights into best practices and potential challenges.

- Interoperability: Ensuring interoperability between different CBDC systems and blockchain platforms is crucial for facilitating seamless cross-border transactions. Standardization of protocols and collaboration between central banks and financial institutions are essential to achieving this interoperability.

- Regulatory Compliance: Clear guidelines and frameworks are needed to define the roles and responsibilities of different stakeholders in the CBDC-based trade finance process. Ensuring compliance with AML, CTF, and other regulatory requirements is essential to maintaining the integrity of the global financial system.

- Privacy and Security: While CBDCs enhance transparency, it is essential to balance this transparency with the need to protect individual privacy and ensure the security of transactions. Robust encryption and authentication measures must be implemented to safeguard against cyberattacks and data breaches.

As the adoption of CBDCs in trade finance continues to grow, continued innovation and collaboration will be key to realizing the full potential of these technologies in transforming global trade and fostering a more inclusive and efficient global economy.

CHAPTER 5:
INSTITUTIONAL
AND INFORMAL
ECONOMIC IMPACTS

5.1 CBDCs and the Role of International Financial Institutions (IFIs)

The emergence of Central Bank Digital Currencies (CBDCs) is poised to redefine the landscape of international finance, influencing the roles and functions of International Financial Institutions (IFIs) such as the International Monetary Fund (IMF), the World Bank, and the Bank for International Settlements (BIS). These institutions play a crucial role in maintaining global financial stability, facilitating international trade, and promoting economic development. CBDCs offer both opportunities and challenges for IFIs as they navigate this evolving financial ecosystem.

The IMF has traditionally been involved in providing financial assistance to countries facing balance of payments crises, offering policy advice, and conducting economic surveillance. With the advent of CBDCs, the IMF's role in advising countries on the design and implementation of digital currencies becomes increasingly important. The institution must develop new frameworks and guidelines to help member countries understand the implications of adopting CBDCs, including their impact on monetary policy, financial stability, and cross-border capital flows. Furthermore, the IMF can facilitate knowledge sharing among countries by documenting best practices and lessons learned from early adopters of CBDCs, thus promoting a more harmonized global approach to digital currency implementation.

The World Bank, which focuses on providing financial and technical assistance to developing countries, can leverage CBDCs to enhance financial inclusion and support economic development. CBDCs have the potential to provide unbanked and underbanked populations with access to secure and efficient digital financial services. The World Bank can assist countries in developing the necessary infrastructure to support CBDC adoption, including digital identification systems, mobile payment platforms, and cybersecurity measures. By promoting the use of CBDCs, the World Bank can help countries reduce the cost of financial transactions, improve the efficiency of public services, and stimulate economic growth.

The BIS, often referred to as the "central bank of central banks," plays a pivotal role in fostering international monetary and financial cooperation. The BIS has been actively involved in researching and analyzing the implications of CBDCs for the global financial system. Through its Innovation Hub, the BIS collaborates with central banks worldwide to explore the potential benefits and risks of CBDCs, develop common standards, and promote interoperability between different digital currency systems. The BIS's work in this area is crucial for ensuring that CBDCs can be integrated seamlessly into the existing global financial infrastructure, minimizing disruptions and enhancing the stability of the international monetary system.

The adoption of CBDCs also presents challenges for IFIs, particularly in the areas of regulatory oversight and coordination. The introduction of digital currencies requires the development of new regulatory frameworks to address issues such as anti-money laundering (AML), counter-terrorism financing (CTF), data privacy, and cybersecurity. IFIs must work closely with national regulators to ensure that these frameworks are robust and consistent across jurisdictions. This coordination is essential to prevent regulatory arbitrage, where entities might exploit differences in regulations between countries to engage in illicit activities.

Another challenge for IFIs is managing the potential impact of CBDCs on the global financial system. The widespread adoption of CBDCs could alter the dynamics of cross-border capital flows, affecting exchange rates, capital controls, and financial stability. IFIs must monitor these developments closely and provide guidance to countries on how to manage the transition to a digital currency environment. This includes advising on measures to mitigate the risks of capital flight, speculative attacks, and other destabilizing activities.

Moreover, the role of IFIs in facilitating international trade could be enhanced by the adoption of CBDCs. Digital currencies can streamline cross-border payments, reducing transaction costs and settlement times. This efficiency can boost international trade by making it easier for businesses to transact across borders. IFIs can support this development by promoting the adoption of CBDCs in international trade agreements and facilitating the integration of digital currencies into global payment systems. Additionally, IFIs can provide technical assistance to countries in developing the necessary infrastructure and regulatory frameworks to support cross-border CBDC transactions.

CBDCs also offer opportunities for improving the transparency and traceability of financial transactions, which can enhance the effectiveness of international aid and development programs. The use of digital currencies can reduce the risk of corruption and fraud by providing a clear and immutable record of transactions. IFIs can leverage this transparency to ensure that funds are used as intended and to enhance the accountability of aid recipients. By incorporating CBDCs into their funding and disbursement mechanisms, IFIs can improve the efficiency and effectiveness of their development initiatives.

Furthermore, the implementation of CBDCs can support the goals of financial stability and economic resilience. Digital currencies can provide central banks with new tools for conducting monetary policy, such as the ability to implement negative interest rates or distribute targeted stimulus payments. IFIs can assist countries in understanding the monetary policy implications of CBDCs and in developing strategies to leverage these new tools effectively. This support is particularly important for developing countries, which may lack the technical expertise and institutional capacity to manage the complexities of digital currency adoption.

The potential for CBDCs to enhance financial inclusion is another area where IFIs can play a significant role. By providing access to secure and efficient digital financial services, CBDCs can help bridge the gap between the formal and informal economies, bringing more people into the financial system. IFIs can support this goal by promoting the development of inclusive digital financial infrastructures and by providing technical assistance to countries in designing and implementing CBDC systems that cater to the needs of underserved populations.

The rise of CBDCs also necessitates a reevaluation of the international monetary system. The dominance of the US dollar as the global reserve currency could be challenged by the adoption of CBDCs by other major economies. This shift could have significant implications for global financial stability and the balance of economic power. IFIs must be prepared to navigate this evolving landscape and provide guidance to countries on how to manage the potential risks and opportunities associated with a more diversified international monetary system.

The emergence of CBDCs presents both opportunities and challenges for International Financial Institutions. By leveraging their expertise and resources, IFIs can play a crucial role in guiding the development and implementation of CBDCs, ensuring that these digital currencies enhance global financial stability, promote economic development, and support financial inclusion. As the global financial system continues to evolve, the collaboration between IFIs, national regulators, and central banks will be essential to realizing the full potential of CBDCs and addressing the complex regulatory, operational, and economic challenges they present.

The transformative potential of CBDCs extends beyond technical and financial aspects, affecting international financial diplomacy and economic policy making at the highest levels. The collaboration among international financial institutions, governments, and regulatory bodies will play a pivotal role in shaping the policies that govern the use of CBDCs across borders.

Global Economic Policy and CBDCs

The integration of CBDCs into global economic policy necessitates a nuanced understanding of macroeconomic dynamics. International Financial Institutions (IFIs) such as the IMF and the World Bank have a critical role to play in advising member countries on the potential macroeconomic implications of CBDCs. These implications include impacts on monetary policy, exchange rates, and global economic stability. For instance, the ability of CBDCs to facilitate easier and more efficient cross-border transactions might influence a country's balance of payments and exchange rate dynamics, requiring new approaches to monetary policy and international economic cooperation.

Standardization and Regulation

A major challenge in the widespread adoption of CBDCs is the need for standardization and consistent regulatory frameworks. IFIs can lead the way in establishing international standards for CBDC transactions, which would help ensure compatibility and interoperability between different national digital currencies. This could involve setting global standards for transaction security, privacy protections, and anti-money laundering practices associated with CBDCs. Achieving this will require an unprecedented level of international cooperation and regulatory alignment, which IFIs are uniquely positioned to facilitate.

Financial Inclusion and Development

CBDCs hold significant promise for enhancing financial inclusion, a primary mandate for many IFIs. By lowering barriers to financial services, CBDCs can provide unbanked or underbanked populations with access to essential financial tools, potentially lifting millions out of poverty and stimulating economic development. International financial institutions can support the deployment of CBDCs in a way that maximizes these inclusive benefits, for instance, by funding the necessary infrastructure in less developed countries or by supporting the development of CBDC platforms that are accessible to people without advanced digital skills or reliable internet access.

Responding to Crises

The potential of CBDCs to provide targeted, efficient, and rapid financial support has implications for how IFIs respond to economic crises. In situations of financial turmoil or natural disasters, CBDCs could be used to quickly distribute aid directly to those affected, bypassing traditional bureaucratic obstacles and delays. IFIs, therefore, need to consider how CBDCs could be integrated into their crisis response strategies, potentially reshaping how global aid is administered.

Ethical and Social Considerations

The adoption of CBDCs also raises significant ethical and social considerations that IFIs must address. These include concerns about privacy, surveillance, and the marginalization of communities that are less digitally literate. IFIs have a responsibility to guide the development of CBDCs in a manner that respects individual rights and promotes social equity. This might involve advocating for privacy safeguards in the design of CBDC systems or supporting education initiatives that ensure all citizens can benefit from digital financial services.

Navigating Geopolitical Implications

The introduction of CBDCs could also have profound geopolitical implications, particularly as major economies like China and the United States explore their own digital currencies. The competitive dynamics of national CBDCs could influence global trade, sanctions policies, and economic alliances. IFIs must be prepared to navigate these complex geopolitical landscapes, promoting cooperation and stability over competition.

Facilitating Sustainable Development

Finally, CBDCs can contribute to sustainable development goals by providing a platform for green finance initiatives. For example, CBDCs could be programmed to support investments in renewable energy projects or to enforce environmental compliance through smart contracts. IFIs can play a crucial role in aligning CBDC policies with broader environmental and sustainability goals, ensuring that the move towards digital currencies also supports global efforts to combat climate change and promote sustainable growth.

The role of International Financial Institutions in the era of

CBDCs is multifaceted and essential. From setting standards and advising on economic policy to promoting financial inclusion and navigating ethical considerations, IFIs are at the forefront of a financial revolution. Their ability to adapt and lead in this new landscape will be crucial in realizing the full potential of CBDCs to contribute to a more inclusive, efficient, and stable global financial system. The future of international finance will likely be marked by increased digitalization, and IFIs will need to evolve accordingly to continue playing a pivotal role in the global economy.

5.2 The Informal Economy: Inclusion and Regulation

The informal economy, comprising activities and income that are partially or fully outside government regulation, oversight, and taxation, plays a crucial role in many countries, especially in developing regions. It includes a wide range of activities, from street vending and small-scale artisanal work to unregistered businesses and services. While the informal sector offers livelihoods to millions of people, it also presents significant challenges in terms of financial inclusion and regulatory oversight. The advent of Central Bank Digital Currencies (CBDCs) offers potential transformative impacts on the informal economy by fostering inclusion and enhancing regulatory capabilities.

5.2.1 Financial Inclusion through CBDCs

CBDCs can dramatically improve financial inclusion for participants in the informal economy. Many individuals engaged in informal activities lack access to traditional banking services due to barriers such as lack of documentation, financial illiteracy, or distrust of formal financial systems. CBDCs, by their nature, can offer a more accessible entry point into the financial system:

- Lower Barriers to Entry: CBDCs can be designed to have lower entry requirements than traditional bank accounts, potentially requiring only a mobile phone to access. This can democratize access to financial services, allowing more people to safely store value, access credit, and make digital payments.
- Ease of Use: With intuitive interfaces and the potential for offline transaction capabilities, CBDC platforms can be tailored to be user-friendly for individuals who are not accustomed to formal banking systems.
- Reduced Costs: By eliminating or reducing transaction fees typically associated with banking and financial services, CBDCs can make everyday financial activities more affordable for informal sector participants.

5.2.2 Enhancing Economic Activity

CBDCs could also enhance economic activity within the informal sector by enabling faster, more secure transactions and providing new mechanisms for credit access:

- Seamless Transactions: CBDCs can facilitate real-time payments with minimal transaction costs, ideal for the high-volume, low-value transactions common in the informal sector.
- Credit Access: With the traceability and data collection capabilities of CBDCs, even informal businesses can establish a verifiable transaction history, potentially opening up new avenues for credit and financial services previously inaccessible.

5.2.3 Regulatory Oversight and Integration

While the informal economy is typically characterized by a lack of regulation and oversight, CBDCs can introduce new ways to integrate informal activities into the formal economy:

- Increased Visibility: Transactions made via CBDCs are recorded on a secure ledger, providing governments with data on economic activities that were previously opaque. This visibility can aid in better economic planning and policy-making.

- Tax Collection: CBDCs can simplify the process of tax collection, making it easier for individuals and businesses in the informal sector to comply with tax regulations. Automated systems can calculate and collect taxes on transactions made with CBDCs, reducing the burden of compliance.
- Legal and Financial Framework: By providing a platform that necessitates certain compliance checks, CBDCs can encourage informal businesses to register and formalize their operations, benefiting from legal protections and services.

5.2.4 Challenges and Considerations

Despite their potential, the introduction of CBDCs in the informal economy faces several challenges:

- Privacy Concerns: The increased visibility of transactions can raise privacy concerns among individuals who rely on the anonymity of cash transactions in the informal economy.
- Technological Barriers: While mobile penetration is high in many developing regions, consistent access to the internet and electricity can be unreliable, potentially limiting the effectiveness of CBDCs.
- Cultural Resistance: There may be resistance from those within the informal sector who distrust digital solutions or governmental oversight, preferring cash for its simplicity and anonymity.

5.2.5 Potential Solutions

Addressing these challenges requires thoughtful implementation and policy frameworks:

- Hybrid Systems: Implementing hybrid systems that allow for offline CBDC transactions can ensure that CBDCs are still usable in areas with intermittent internet access.
- Education and Outreach: Educational campaigns and outreach programs can help demystify CBDCs and demonstrate their benefits over cash, particularly in terms of security and

convenience.

- Balancing Oversight with Privacy: Developing privacy-preserving features within the CBDC architecture can help balance the need for regulatory oversight with individual privacy concerns.

CBDCs hold significant potential to transform the informal economy by enhancing financial inclusion, increasing economic activity, and improving regulatory oversight. However, their successful implementation will depend on addressing technological, cultural, and operational challenges. With careful planning and commitment, CBDCs could bridge the gap between the formal and informal economies, fostering broader economic participation and growth.

5.3 CBDCs and Financial Inclusion Initiatives

Financial inclusion is the cornerstone of economic development, aiming to provide all individuals and businesses access to useful and affordable financial products and services that meet their needs. Central Bank Digital Currencies (CBDCs) have the potential to significantly enhance financial inclusion, particularly in underserved and marginalized communities. This section explores how CBDCs can support financial inclusion initiatives, discussing their potential benefits, implementation strategies, and the challenges that need to be addressed.

5.3.1 Enhancing Access to Financial Services

CBDCs can play a pivotal role in bridging the financial inclusion gap by providing a more accessible and user-friendly entry point into the financial system. Traditional banking services often pose barriers to entry for individuals without formal identification, stable income, or credit history. CBDCs can help overcome these barriers by leveraging digital technology to provide inclusive financial services.

- Simplified Account Opening: CBDCs can streamline the process of opening accounts, reducing the need for extensive documentation and credit checks. Digital identification systems linked to CBDC wallets can facilitate easier access for those without formal IDs.
- Mobile-First Solutions: With the widespread adoption of mobile phones, especially in developing regions, CBDCs can be integrated into mobile payment platforms. This enables users to conduct transactions, store value, and access financial services through their mobile devices, even without access to traditional banking infrastructure.
- Cost-Effective Transactions: By reducing transaction fees and eliminating intermediaries, CBDCs can make financial services more affordable for low-income individuals. This affordability can encourage more people to participate in the formal financial system.

5.3.2 Empowering Women and Marginalized Groups

CBDCs have the potential to empower women and marginalized groups who often face greater barriers to financial inclusion. These groups can benefit from the enhanced security, privacy, and convenience offered by digital currencies.

- Secure and Private Transactions: Women and marginalized individuals can use CBDCs to conduct secure and private transactions, reducing the risk of theft and exploitation. The digital nature of CBDCs can also provide a safer alternative to carrying cash.
- Economic Empowerment: Access to CBDCs can enable women and marginalized groups to participate more fully in the economy, whether through entrepreneurship, employment, or investment. Digital financial tools can help them save, invest, and grow their wealth.
- Social and Economic Mobility: By providing access to financial services, CBDCs can support social and economic mobility,

allowing individuals to improve their standard of living and achieve financial independence.

5.3.3 Supporting Microfinance and Small Businesses

Microfinance institutions and small businesses play a crucial role in promoting financial inclusion by providing credit and financial services to underserved populations. CBDCs can enhance the effectiveness of these institutions and support the growth of small businesses.

- Efficient Microfinance Operations: CBDCs can streamline the operations of microfinance institutions by automating loan disbursements, repayments, and record-keeping. This efficiency can reduce operational costs and improve service delivery.
- Access to Credit: Small businesses can benefit from the transparency and traceability of CBDC transactions, which can help build credit histories and improve access to formal credit. Lenders can use this transaction data to assess creditworthiness more accurately.
- Integration with Supply Chains: CBDCs can facilitate seamless integration with supply chains, enabling small businesses to conduct transactions with suppliers and customers more efficiently. This can enhance cash flow management and business growth.

5.3.4 Digital Literacy and Financial Education

While CBDCs offer significant potential for enhancing financial inclusion, their successful implementation requires a focus on digital literacy and financial education. Ensuring that users understand how to use digital financial tools safely and effectively is essential.

- Digital Literacy Programs: Governments and financial institutions can implement digital literacy programs to educate individuals about the benefits and usage of CBDCs. These programs can cover topics such as digital security, mobile banking, and financial management.

- Financial Education Initiatives: Financial education initiatives can help users understand the broader financial landscape, including budgeting, saving, and investing. By equipping individuals with financial knowledge, these initiatives can promote responsible financial behavior and long-term financial health.

5.3.5 Addressing Challenges and Barriers

While CBDCs hold significant promise for enhancing financial inclusion, several challenges and barriers need to be addressed to ensure their successful implementation.

- Technological Infrastructure: The availability of reliable technological infrastructure, including internet connectivity and mobile networks, is crucial for the effective use of CBDCs. Investments in digital infrastructure are necessary to support widespread access.
- Privacy and Security Concerns: Ensuring the privacy and security of CBDC transactions is essential to gain the trust of users. Robust encryption, authentication, and anti-fraud measures must be implemented to protect users' financial data.
- Regulatory Frameworks: Clear regulatory frameworks are needed to govern the use of CBDCs, protect consumers, and prevent illicit activities. Collaboration between central banks, financial institutions, and regulatory bodies is essential to develop and enforce these frameworks.
- User Trust and Acceptance: Building trust and acceptance among users is critical for the adoption of CBDCs. Transparent communication, user-friendly interfaces, and reliable service delivery can help build confidence in digital currencies.

5.3.6 Case Studies: CBDCs in Financial Inclusion Initiatives

Several countries and organizations are exploring the use of CBDCs to promote financial inclusion. These case studies provide valuable insights into the practical applications and benefits of CBDCs in enhancing financial inclusion.

- The Bahamas' Sand Dollar: The Central Bank of The Bahamas launched the Sand Dollar, one of the first fully operational retail CBDCs, to promote financial inclusion. The Sand Dollar provides a secure and efficient means of payment for individuals and businesses, particularly in remote areas with limited access to traditional banking services.
- Cambodia's Project Bakong: Cambodia's Project Bakong is a blockchain-based payment system that aims to enhance financial inclusion by providing digital financial services to underserved populations. The system integrates with mobile payment platforms, enabling users to conduct transactions and access financial services through their mobile phones.
- Nigeria's eNaira: The Central Bank of Nigeria introduced the eNaira to enhance financial inclusion and support economic development. The eNaira aims to provide a secure and efficient digital payment solution, particularly for the unbanked and underbanked populations in Nigeria.

CBDCs hold significant potential to enhance financial inclusion by providing accessible, affordable, and secure financial services to underserved and marginalized communities. By addressing the challenges and barriers to implementation, governments and financial institutions can leverage CBDCs to promote economic empowerment, support small businesses, and foster social and economic mobility. The successful integration of CBDCs into financial inclusion initiatives requires a collaborative effort, focusing on digital literacy, regulatory frameworks, and user trust to realize the full potential of digital currencies in creating a more inclusive and equitable financial system.

5.4 Case Studies: Integrating Informal Economies

The integration of informal economies into the formal financial system has long been a challenge for policymakers and financial institutions. Central Bank Digital Currencies (CBDCs) offer a novel approach to addressing this issue by providing a secure, transparent, and efficient platform for economic transactions. This section explores various case studies that highlight the potential of CBDCs to integrate informal economies, showcasing the benefits and challenges of implementing such digital currencies in diverse contexts.

Case Study 1: The Sand Dollar in The Bahamas

The Sand Dollar, launched by the Central Bank of The Bahamas, serves as one of the pioneering examples of a CBDC aimed at enhancing financial inclusion and integrating the informal economy. The Bahamas consists of many islands, making it difficult for traditional banking infrastructure to reach all inhabitants. The Sand Dollar addresses this challenge by providing a digital currency accessible via mobile phones.

The integration of the Sand Dollar into the Bahamian economy has shown promising results. Informal vendors, fishermen, and small business owners now use the Sand Dollar to conduct transactions, reducing their reliance on cash. This digital currency has facilitated easier and faster payments, increased transaction security, and provided a transparent record of economic activities, which can help informal businesses build credit histories.

The Sand Dollar's implementation faced challenges, such as ensuring widespread adoption and addressing digital literacy issues. However, through targeted outreach and education programs, the Central Bank of The Bahamas has successfully promoted the use of the Sand Dollar, enhancing economic participation and financial inclusion across the islands.

Case Study 2: Project Bakong in Cambodia

Cambodia's Project Bakong is a blockchain-based payment system developed by the National Bank of Cambodia. While not a CBDC in the strictest sense, Bakong functions similarly by providing a digital platform for financial transactions. The project aims to enhance financial inclusion and integrate the country's largely cash-based informal economy.

Bakong allows users to make payments and transfer money using their mobile phones, even without a traditional bank account. This accessibility has been particularly beneficial for rural populations and small-scale traders who previously relied on cash transactions. By providing a secure and efficient payment system, Bakong has helped reduce the risks associated with carrying and storing cash, such as theft and loss.

The project's success in integrating the informal economy can be attributed to its user-friendly interface and the collaboration with local financial institutions and mobile operators. This cooperation has ensured that Bakong is widely accepted and used across the country, facilitating the transition from a cash-based to a digital economy.

Case Study 3: India's Digital Payment Ecosystem

India's digital payment ecosystem, bolstered by the Unified Payments Interface (UPI) and the Aadhaar biometric identification system, offers valuable insights into integrating informal economies through digital financial solutions. While India has not yet launched a CBDC, the existing digital infrastructure provides a strong foundation for such an initiative.

UPI allows users to link their bank accounts to a mobile app, enabling instant and secure transactions. This system has been instrumental in bringing millions of Indians into the formal financial system, including those operating in the informal economy. Street vendors, small retailers, and gig workers can now accept digital payments, reducing their dependence on cash.

The integration of UPI with Aadhaar has further enhanced financial inclusion by simplifying the process of opening bank accounts and accessing financial services. By leveraging these digital tools, India has made significant strides in formalizing its informal economy, providing a blueprint for how CBDCs could be used to achieve similar outcomes.

Case Study 4: Nigeria's eNaira

The Central Bank of Nigeria launched the eNaira as part of its efforts to promote financial inclusion and integrate the informal economy. Nigeria has a large informal sector, with many transactions conducted in cash. The eNaira aims to address this by providing a secure and efficient digital payment solution.

The eNaira can be accessed via a mobile app, allowing users to make payments, transfer money, and store value digitally. This digital currency has been particularly beneficial for small business owners, market traders, and rural populations who previously had limited access to formal financial services. By facilitating digital transactions, the eNaira has reduced the costs and risks associated with cash handling.

The Central Bank of Nigeria has undertaken extensive public awareness campaigns and partnered with local financial institutions to promote the adoption of the eNaira. These efforts have been crucial in overcoming initial resistance and ensuring that the digital currency is widely accepted and used across the country.

Case Study 5: Brazil's Pix Payment System

Brazil's Pix payment system, developed by the Central Bank of Brazil, provides another example of integrating the informal economy through digital financial solutions. While not a CBDC, Pix is a real-time payment platform that enables instant and secure transactions using mobile phones, QR codes, and internet banking.

Pix has been widely adopted in Brazil, with millions of users and thousands of businesses accepting Pix payments. This system has been particularly beneficial for informal workers, street vendors, and small retailers, allowing them to receive payments digitally and securely. The transparency and efficiency of Pix transactions have helped build trust and reduce the reliance on cash.

The success of Pix can be attributed to its ease of use, widespread acceptance, and the Central Bank of Brazil's efforts to promote financial inclusion. By providing a digital payment solution that is accessible to all, Pix has facilitated the integration of the informal economy into the formal financial system.

Case Study 6: China's Digital Yuan

China's digital yuan, also known as the Digital Currency Electronic Payment (DCEP), represents one of the most advanced CBDC initiatives globally. The People's Bank of China (PBOC) has conducted extensive pilot programs to test the digital yuan's capabilities in various settings, including its potential to integrate the informal economy.

The digital yuan can be used for everyday transactions through mobile apps, providing a convenient and secure alternative to cash. Street vendors, small businesses, and rural populations have participated in these pilots, demonstrating the digital yuan's potential to enhance financial inclusion and economic activity.

The PBOC has focused on ensuring that the digital yuan is user-friendly and widely accepted, collaborating with commercial banks and payment service providers. The pilot programs have shown that the digital yuan can reduce transaction costs, enhance security, and provide valuable data for economic planning and policy-making.

These case studies illustrate the diverse approaches and benefits of integrating informal economies through digital financial solutions, including CBDCs. By providing accessible, secure, and efficient payment platforms, CBDCs can enhance financial inclusion, reduce the risks associated with cash transactions, and promote economic participation. The success of these initiatives depends on thoughtful implementation, collaboration with local stakeholders, and addressing challenges such as digital literacy and infrastructure. As more countries explore and adopt CBDCs, these case studies offer valuable lessons and insights into the potential of digital currencies to transform informal economies and foster inclusive economic growth.

The successful integration of informal economies with formal financial systems through the use of CBDCs requires an understanding of the unique characteristics and challenges associated with these economies. The following additional case studies further illustrate how CBDCs can bridge the gap between informal and formal financial sectors, facilitating economic growth and financial inclusion.

Case Study 7: Kenya's M-Pesa and Potential CBDC Integration

Kenya's M-Pesa, a mobile money platform launched by Safaricom, has revolutionized financial inclusion in the country. While M-Pesa itself is not a CBDC, its success in integrating the informal economy provides a compelling case for how a CBDC could further enhance financial inclusion.

M-Pesa allows users to deposit, withdraw, transfer money, and pay for goods and services using a mobile phone. It has been particularly beneficial for informal sector workers, such as small-scale farmers, market traders, and urban migrants, providing them with a secure and efficient way to manage their finances.

The potential integration of a Kenyan CBDC with the existing M-Pesa platform could amplify these benefits. A CBDC could provide a more stable and government-backed digital currency option, reducing reliance on cash and further increasing the transparency and efficiency of transactions. This integration could also facilitate better regulatory oversight and reduce the risks associated with unregulated digital money platforms.

Case Study 8: South Africa's Project Khokha

South Africa's Project Khokha is an initiative by the South African Reserve Bank (SARB) to explore the potential of distributed ledger technology (DLT) for wholesale payments. Although primarily focused on interbank settlements, the principles and learnings from Project Khokha can be applied to the broader financial inclusion agenda, including the informal economy.

Project Khokha demonstrated the potential for DLT to provide real-time, secure, and cost-effective payment solutions. If these technologies were adapted for retail use, particularly in a CBDC context, they could significantly enhance the integration of South Africa's large informal economy.

A South African CBDC could build on the success of Project Khokha by providing informal workers and small businesses with access to a reliable and efficient payment system. This could reduce the risks associated with cash handling and improve access to financial services, helping to formalize the informal economy and increase economic participation.

Case Study 9: Peru's Financial Inclusion Strategy with Potential CBDC Adoption

Peru has made significant strides in financial inclusion through initiatives such as its National Financial Inclusion Strategy (NFIS). The introduction of a Peruvian CBDC could further these efforts by providing a digital platform that reaches underserved populations in both urban and rural areas.

Peru's informal economy is substantial, encompassing a wide range of activities from agriculture to small-scale retail. A CBDC could provide these informal workers with a secure and efficient way to conduct transactions, save money, and access credit. By reducing reliance on cash, a CBDC could also help mitigate the risks of theft and fraud, which are prevalent in cash-based transactions.

The Peruvian government could leverage existing financial inclusion initiatives, such as the expansion of mobile banking and digital payment systems, to promote the adoption of a CBDC. Educational campaigns and partnerships with local financial institutions would be crucial to ensure that the benefits of a CBDC are accessible to all segments of the population.

Case Study 10: Mexico's Digital Peso Initiative

Mexico is exploring the potential of a digital peso to enhance financial inclusion and integrate its informal economy. The country has a significant informal sector, with many workers lacking access to traditional banking services. A digital peso could provide a secure and efficient means of payment, fostering greater economic participation.

The Mexican government has initiated several pilot programs to test the digital peso in various contexts, including informal markets and rural areas. These pilots have shown that a digital currency can reduce transaction costs, increase security, and provide a transparent record of economic activities.

The integration of the digital peso with existing mobile payment platforms and financial inclusion programs could further enhance its impact. By providing informal workers and small businesses with access to digital financial services, the digital peso could help formalize the informal economy and support

116

economic growth.

Case Study 11: Indonesia's Rupiah Digital Initiative

Indonesia's central bank, Bank Indonesia, has been exploring the development of a digital rupiah as part of its efforts to enhance financial inclusion and integrate the informal economy. Indonesia's vast archipelago and diverse population present unique challenges for financial inclusion, with many regions lacking access to traditional banking services.

The digital rupiah aims to address these challenges by providing a secure and accessible digital payment platform. Pilot programs in various regions have demonstrated the potential of the digital rupiah to reduce transaction costs, increase security, and enhance transparency in economic transactions.

The successful implementation of a digital rupiah would require collaboration with local financial institutions, mobile network operators, and community organizations to ensure widespread adoption. Educational initiatives and user-friendly interfaces would be crucial to ensure that the benefits of the digital rupiah are accessible to all segments of the population.

Case Study 12: Ethiopia's Digital Birr Exploration

Ethiopia is exploring the development of a digital birr to enhance financial inclusion and integrate its informal economy. The country's large informal sector and low levels of financial inclusion present significant challenges for economic development.

A digital birr could provide a secure and efficient means of payment for informal workers and small businesses, reducing reliance on cash and improving access to financial services. Pilot programs in urban and rural areas have shown that a digital currency can enhance transaction efficiency, increase security, and provide a transparent record of economic activities.

The Ethiopian government's efforts to promote the digital birr include partnerships with local financial institutions and mobile network operators, as well as educational campaigns to increase digital literacy. By leveraging these initiatives, Ethiopia aims to integrate its informal economy into the formal financial system, supporting economic growth and development.

These case studies illustrate the diverse approaches and benefits of integrating informal economies through the use of CBDCs. By providing accessible, secure, and efficient payment platforms, CBDCs can enhance financial inclusion, reduce the risks associated with cash transactions, and promote economic participation. The successful integration of informal economies with formal financial systems requires thoughtful implementation, collaboration with local stakeholders, and addressing challenges such as digital literacy and infrastructure. As more countries explore and adopt CBDCs, these case studies offer valuable lessons and insights into the potential of digital currencies to transform informal economies and foster inclusive economic growth.

CHAPTER 6:
FINANCIAL STABILITY
IN THE DIGITAL AGE
6.1 The Role of CBDCs in Financial Stability

Central Bank Digital Currencies (CBDCs) have the potential to play a significant role in maintaining and enhancing financial stability in the digital age. As financial systems become increasingly digital, CBDCs offer a new tool for central banks to ensure the smooth functioning of financial markets, prevent systemic risks, and promote economic resilience. This section explores how CBDCs can contribute to financial stability, examining their impact on monetary policy, financial institutions, and the broader financial ecosystem.

CBDCs and Monetary Policy

CBDCs provide central banks with new mechanisms to implement and transmit monetary policy more effectively. Traditional monetary policy tools, such as interest rates and reserve requirements, can be complemented by the unique features of CBDCs.

- Enhanced Control Over Money Supply: CBDCs allow central banks to have direct control over the money supply, enabling more precise adjustments to liquidity in the economy. This can be particularly useful in times of economic stress, where swift and targeted interventions are necessary.

- Negative Interest Rates: With cash, it is difficult to implement negative interest rates because individuals can simply hold physical currency to avoid paying interest. CBDCs, however, can be designed to support negative interest rates, providing central banks with additional flexibility in managing economic downturns.

- Direct Transmission of Policy: CBDCs enable direct distribution of stimulus payments or other monetary policy measures to individuals and businesses. This direct transmission can increase the effectiveness and speed of policy implementation, ensuring that the intended economic impact is achieved.

Strengthening Financial Institutions

The introduction of CBDCs can influence the stability and resilience of financial institutions by changing the dynamics of banking and payment systems.

- Reduced Risk of Bank Runs: CBDCs can provide a safer alternative to bank deposits, potentially reducing the risk of bank runs. In times of financial instability, individuals might prefer to hold CBDCs, which are backed by the central bank, rather than commercial bank deposits. This can alleviate pressure on banks and enhance overall financial stability.

- Efficient Payment Systems: CBDCs can modernize payment systems, making them more efficient and resilient. By reducing reliance on traditional banking infrastructure and intermediaries, CBDCs can lower transaction costs, enhance security, and increase the speed of financial transactions. This efficiency can contribute to the stability of financial institutions and the broader economy.

- Improved Transparency: The use of blockchain technology in CBDCs ensures that all transactions are recorded in an immutable ledger, providing greater transparency. This transparency can help regulators monitor financial institutions more effectively, identify potential risks, and take preventive measures to maintain stability.

Mitigating Systemic Risks

CBDCs can help mitigate systemic risks that threaten the stability of the financial system. These risks include cyber threats, fraud, and the interconnectedness of financial institutions.

- Cybersecurity: The digital nature of CBDCs necessitates robust cybersecurity measures to protect against cyberattacks. By implementing advanced encryption and authentication protocols, central banks can ensure the security of CBDC transactions. This enhanced cybersecurity can reduce the risk of large-scale financial disruptions caused by cyber threats.
- Fraud Prevention: The transparency and traceability of CBDC transactions can help prevent fraud and financial crimes. Each transaction is recorded on a blockchain, providing a clear and tamper-proof audit trail. This can help regulators and law enforcement agencies detect and prevent fraudulent activities, contributing to the overall stability of the financial system.
- Reduced Interconnectedness: The use of CBDCs can reduce the interconnectedness of financial institutions by providing a direct means of transaction between parties. This can limit the contagion effect in times of financial stress, where the failure of one institution can trigger a cascade of failures across the financial system.

CBDCs and Financial Market Infrastructure

CBDCs have the potential to enhance the resilience and stability of financial market infrastructure, including payment systems, clearinghouses, and settlement systems.

- Resilient Payment Systems: CBDCs can provide a more resilient and efficient payment system, reducing the risk of disruptions. By leveraging distributed ledger technology, CBDCs can ensure continuous operation even in the face of technical failures or cyberattacks. This resilience can enhance the stability of the financial market infrastructure.

- Efficient Clearing and Settlement: The use of CBDCs can streamline clearing and settlement processes, reducing the time and costs associated with these activities. This efficiency can improve the functioning of financial markets, reduce counterparty risk, and enhance overall stability.
- Cross-Border Payments: CBDCs can facilitate more efficient and secure cross-border payments, reducing the risk of disruptions in international financial flows. By providing a standardized and interoperable digital currency, CBDCs can enhance the stability of global financial markets.

Challenges and Considerations

While CBDCs offer significant potential for enhancing financial stability, their implementation also presents challenges that need to be addressed.

- Design and Implementation: The design of CBDCs must balance the need for security, privacy, and efficiency. Central banks must carefully consider the technical and operational aspects of CBDCs to ensure they are robust and reliable.
- Regulatory Frameworks: Clear regulatory frameworks are essential to govern the use of CBDCs and ensure their integration into the existing financial system. This includes addressing issues related to anti-money laundering (AML), counter-terrorism financing (CTF), and consumer protection.
- Financial Stability Risks: The introduction of CBDCs could pose risks to financial stability, such as disintermediation of banks and increased volatility in financial markets. Central banks must carefully manage these risks to ensure the stability of the financial system.
- Public Trust and Adoption: The success of CBDCs depends on public trust and widespread adoption. Central banks must engage with stakeholders, including the public, financial

institutions, and policymakers, to build confidence in CBDCs and promote their use.

CBDCs have the potential to play a crucial role in enhancing financial stability in the digital age. By providing new tools for monetary policy, strengthening financial institutions, mitigating systemic risks, and improving financial market infrastructure, CBDCs can contribute to a more resilient and stable financial system. However, the successful implementation of CBDCs requires careful consideration of design, regulatory, and operational challenges. Central banks must navigate these challenges to harness the full potential of CBDCs in promoting financial stability and supporting economic growth.

6.2 Mitigating Financial Crises with Digital Currencies

Central Bank Digital Currencies (CBDCs) offer new mechanisms for mitigating financial crises by enhancing the tools available to central banks, improving the efficiency and transparency of financial transactions, and providing a stable medium of exchange during periods of economic instability. This section explores how CBDCs can be leveraged to prevent, manage, and recover from financial crises, addressing the unique challenges posed by modern financial systems.

Preventing Financial Crises

CBDCs can play a crucial role in preventing financial crises through their impact on monetary policy, financial supervision, and systemic risk management.

Enhanced Monetary Policy Tools: CBDCs provide central banks with more precise tools for managing the money supply and implementing monetary policy. The ability to directly control the issuance and circulation of digital currency allows for more targeted interventions. For example, central banks can quickly adjust the money supply in response to economic indicators, preventing the build-up of imbalances that could lead to a crisis.

Improved Financial Supervision: The transparency and traceability of CBDC transactions enable more effective monitoring and supervision of financial institutions. Regulators can gain real-time insights into the flow of funds, identify emerging risks, and take preemptive measures to address potential vulnerabilities. This proactive approach can help prevent the conditions that lead to financial crises.

Managing Financial Crises

In the event of a financial crisis, CBDCs offer several advantages for managing and mitigating the impact of the crisis on the economy.

Direct Stimulus Distribution: During a financial crisis, central banks and governments often need to provide stimulus payments to individuals and businesses to support economic activity. CBDCs facilitate the direct and instantaneous distribution of these payments, ensuring that financial support reaches those in need without delay. This efficiency can help stabilize consumption and investment, mitigating the depth and duration of the crisis.

Liquidity Support: CBDCs can provide a reliable source of liquidity during times of financial stress. Central banks can use CBDCs to inject liquidity into the financial system, ensuring that financial institutions have the funds necessary to meet their obligations. This can prevent liquidity shortages from escalating into broader solvency problems, stabilizing the financial system.

Preventing Bank Runs: One of the risks during a financial crisis is a run on banks, where depositors withdraw their funds en masse, fearing that the bank may become insolvent. CBDCs, as a digital form of central bank money, can provide a safe and stable alternative to bank deposits. The assurance of central bank backing can reduce the likelihood of bank runs, maintaining stability in the banking sector.

Recovery from Financial Crises

CBDCs can also play a significant role in the recovery phase following a financial crisis, supporting economic rebuilding and long-term stability.

Facilitating Economic Activity: By providing a secure and efficient payment infrastructure, CBDCs can facilitate economic transactions and support the recovery of businesses and households. The reduced transaction costs and increased speed of CBDC payments can stimulate economic activity, helping the economy to rebound more quickly.

Restoring Confidence: The transparency and traceability of CBDC transactions can help restore confidence in the financial system. Clear records of transactions and the ability to track the flow of funds can reassure stakeholders that financial activities are being monitored and regulated effectively. This transparency can rebuild trust among investors, businesses, and consumers, which is essential for a sustained recovery.

Supporting Long-Term Stability: The data generated by CBDC transactions can provide valuable insights for policymakers, helping them to identify trends, assess risks, and develop strategies for long-term economic stability. The continuous feedback loop created by CBDC data can improve the responsiveness and effectiveness of economic policies, reducing the likelihood of future crises.

Case Studies: CBDCs in Action During Financial Crises

Several pilot projects and initiatives have explored the use of CBDCs in mitigating financial crises, providing valuable lessons for future implementations.

China's Digital Yuan: During the COVID-19 pandemic, China accelerated the testing and deployment of its digital yuan. The digital currency was used to distribute emergency payments and subsidies directly to individuals and businesses affected by the pandemic. This direct distribution helped stabilize consumption and provided much-needed support to the economy during a period of significant disruption.

Bahamas' Sand Dollar: The Bahamas has leveraged its Sand Dollar CBDC to enhance financial resilience in the face of natural disasters. The digital currency has been used to provide rapid financial assistance to citizens affected by hurricanes and other emergencies, ensuring that aid reaches those in need quickly and efficiently. This experience highlights the potential of CBDCs to support recovery efforts in the aftermath of crises.

Sweden's e-Krona: Sweden's e-Krona project explores the use of digital currency to enhance financial stability and resilience. The e-Krona aims to provide a stable and secure payment option that can be relied upon during periods of financial stress. The project includes simulations of financial crisis scenarios to test the effectiveness of the e-Krona in maintaining liquidity and supporting economic activity.

Challenges and Considerations

While CBDCs offer significant potential for mitigating financial crises, several challenges and considerations must be addressed to ensure their effective implementation.

Technology and Infrastructure: The development and deployment of CBDCs require robust technological infrastructure. Ensuring the security, scalability, and reliability of the digital currency system is essential for its success. Central banks must invest in advanced technologies and cybersecurity measures to protect against cyber threats and ensure the smooth functioning of CBDCs.

Regulatory Frameworks: The introduction of CBDCs necessitates clear and comprehensive regulatory frameworks. Central banks and policymakers must establish guidelines for the issuance, distribution, and use of CBDCs, addressing issues such as anti-money laundering (AML), counter-terrorism financing (CTF), and consumer protection. These frameworks must be adaptable to evolving technological and economic conditions.

Public Trust and Adoption: The success of CBDCs depends on public trust and widespread adoption. Central banks must engage in transparent communication and education efforts to build confidence in the digital currency. Ensuring that CBDCs are user-friendly and accessible to all segments of the population is crucial for achieving broad acceptance.

CBDCs hold significant potential for mitigating financial crises by enhancing monetary policy tools, improving financial supervision, providing liquidity support, and facilitating economic recovery. The successful implementation of CBDCs requires careful consideration of technological, regulatory, and public trust factors. By leveraging the unique features of digital currencies, central banks can strengthen financial stability and resilience, supporting sustainable economic growth in the digital age.

6.3 CBDCs and Systemic Risk Management

Central Bank Digital Currencies (CBDCs) offer promising tools for systemic risk management in an increasingly digital and interconnected financial landscape. By providing enhanced transparency, improving the efficiency of payment systems, and offering new mechanisms for liquidity provision, CBDCs can help mitigate systemic risks and ensure the stability of the financial system. This section explores how CBDCs can contribute to systemic risk management and highlights key strategies for their effective implementation.

Improving Transparency and Traceability

One of the primary benefits of CBDCs is their ability to improve transparency and traceability in financial transactions. By recording all transactions on a blockchain or distributed ledger, CBDCs create a permanent and immutable record of economic activity. This transparency can help regulators and central banks monitor the financial system more effectively and identify emerging risks before they become systemic issues.

For instance, during periods of financial instability, the transparent nature of CBDC transactions can provide real-time data on capital flows, helping authorities detect unusual patterns or spikes in withdrawals that could indicate stress in the financial system. This early warning system allows for timely interventions to stabilize markets and prevent contagion.

Enhancing Payment System Resilience

CBDCs can enhance the resilience of payment systems by reducing reliance on traditional banking infrastructure and intermediaries. The decentralized nature of blockchain technology ensures that payment systems remain operational even in the face of technical failures or cyberattacks. This resilience is crucial for maintaining confidence in the financial system and ensuring the continuity of economic activity during crises.

By providing a secure and efficient alternative to traditional payment systems, CBDCs can also reduce settlement times and lower transaction costs. This efficiency can mitigate systemic risks by enhancing liquidity and reducing the likelihood of payment delays or failures that could trigger broader financial instability.

Providing Liquidity and Stability

In times of financial stress, the ability to provide liquidity quickly and effectively is essential for maintaining financial stability. CBDCs offer central banks a powerful tool for liquidity provision, enabling them to inject funds directly into the financial system without relying on intermediary banks.

For example, during a financial crisis, central banks can use CBDCs to provide emergency liquidity to financial institutions facing liquidity shortages. This direct intervention can prevent liquidity crises from escalating into solvency crises, stabilizing the financial system and maintaining the flow of credit to the real economy.

CBDCs can also facilitate more targeted and efficient monetary policy interventions. By enabling direct transfers to individuals and businesses, CBDCs can enhance the effectiveness of fiscal stimulus measures and support economic recovery more effectively than traditional methods.

Strengthening Regulatory Oversight

CBDCs provide regulators with powerful tools for enhancing oversight and ensuring compliance with financial regulations. The transparent and traceable nature of CBDC transactions allows regulators to monitor financial activities in real-time, identify potential risks, and enforce compliance with anti-money laundering (AML) and counter-terrorism financing (CTF) regulations.

By providing detailed transaction data, CBDCs can help regulators detect and prevent fraudulent activities, such as money laundering and terrorist financing. This enhanced oversight can reduce systemic risks associated with financial crimes and increase the overall stability of the financial system.

Supporting Financial Inclusion and Stability

Financial inclusion is a key component of financial stability, as it ensures that all segments of the population have access to secure and reliable financial services. CBDCs can play a significant role in promoting financial inclusion by providing accessible and affordable digital financial services to underserved and unbanked populations.

By reducing barriers to entry and lowering transaction costs, CBDCs can encourage greater participation in the formal financial system. This increased inclusion can enhance economic resilience and stability by broadening the base of financial participants and reducing reliance on informal and unregulated financial activities.

Challenges and Considerations

While CBDCs offer significant potential for systemic risk management, their implementation also presents challenges that need to be carefully addressed:

Technological and Operational Risks: The development and deployment of CBDCs require robust technological infrastructure and cybersecurity measures. Ensuring the security, scalability, and reliability of CBDC systems is essential for preventing cyber threats and operational failures that could undermine financial stability.

Regulatory Coordination: The introduction of CBDCs necessitates coordination between central banks, financial institutions, and regulatory bodies. Establishing clear and comprehensive regulatory frameworks is crucial for governing the use of CBDCs, ensuring compliance, and addressing cross-border issues.

Interoperability and Integration: CBDCs must be designed to be interoperable with existing financial systems and international payment networks. Ensuring seamless integration and compatibility with other digital currencies and payment platforms is essential for maintaining the efficiency and stability of the global financial system.

Public Trust and Adoption: Building public trust and encouraging widespread adoption of CBDCs is critical for their success. Transparent communication, user-friendly interfaces, and reliable service delivery are key factors in gaining public confidence and ensuring that CBDCs are widely used.

Case Studies: Systemic Risk Management with CBDCs

Several countries and central banks are exploring the use of CBDCs for systemic risk management, providing valuable insights into their potential applications and benefits:

The Digital Euro Project: The European Central Bank (ECB) is exploring the development of a digital euro to enhance the stability and resilience of the eurozone's financial system. The digital euro aims to provide a secure and efficient means of payment, support financial inclusion, and improve the effectiveness of monetary policy. Pilot programs and simulations are being conducted to assess the impact of the digital euro on financial stability and systemic risk management.

Singapore's Project Ubin: The Monetary Authority of Singapore (MAS) has conducted several phases of Project Ubin, exploring the use of blockchain technology for interbank payments and settlements. The project has demonstrated the potential of CBDCs to enhance payment system resilience, reduce settlement times, and lower transaction costs. By improving the efficiency and security of the financial system, Project Ubin contributes to systemic risk management and financial stability.

Canada's Project Jasper: The Bank of Canada has undertaken Project Jasper to explore the use of distributed ledger technology (DLT) for wholesale payments. The project has shown that CBDCs can provide a more resilient and efficient payment infrastructure, reducing systemic risks and enhancing financial stability. The lessons learned from Project Jasper are being used to inform the design and implementation of potential future CBDCs.

The potential of CBDCs to enhance systemic risk management and financial stability is significant. However, realizing this potential requires careful consideration of design, regulatory, and operational challenges. Central banks must navigate these complexities to harness the full benefits of CBDCs and ensure their successful implementation.

As more countries explore and adopt CBDCs, the insights gained from pilot projects and early implementations will provide valuable lessons for future developments. Continued innovation, collaboration, and coordination among central banks, financial institutions, and regulators will be essential for leveraging CBDCs to create a more resilient and stable global financial system.

CBDCs offer promising tools for systemic risk management in the digital age. By improving transparency, enhancing payment system resilience, providing liquidity support, and strengthening regulatory oversight, CBDCs can contribute to a more stable and resilient financial system. The successful implementation of CBDCs requires addressing technological, regulatory, and public trust challenges, but with careful planning and coordination, CBDCs can play a crucial role in promoting financial stability and supporting sustainable economic growth.

6.4 CBDCs and Monetary Policy: Opportunities and Challenges

Central Bank Digital Currencies (CBDCs) offer unique opportunities for enhancing the effectiveness of monetary policy. At the same time, their introduction presents significant challenges that central banks must address to ensure a smooth transition and maintain economic stability. This section explores how CBDCs can influence monetary policy, examining both the opportunities they present and the challenges they pose.

Opportunities for Monetary Policy with CBDCs

Enhanced Precision and Control: CBDCs provide central banks with the ability to implement monetary policy measures with greater precision and control. Unlike traditional forms of money, CBDCs can be programmed to have specific characteristics, such as expiration dates for stimulus payments or tiered interest rates for different types of accounts. This programmability allows central banks to tailor monetary policy interventions more effectively to achieve desired economic outcomes.

Direct Policy Transmission: CBDCs enable direct transmission of monetary policy measures to individuals and businesses. For example, during an economic downturn, central banks can distribute stimulus payments directly to citizens' CBDC wallets, ensuring that the intended economic support reaches the target population quickly and efficiently. This direct approach can enhance the effectiveness of monetary policy, particularly in times of crisis.

Negative Interest Rates: Implementing negative interest rates in a traditional banking system is challenging because individuals and businesses can withdraw cash to avoid paying interest. With CBDCs, central banks can impose negative interest rates directly on digital currency holdings, providing a more effective tool for stimulating spending and investment during periods of economic stagnation.

Real-Time Economic Data: The use of CBDCs generates real-time data on economic transactions, providing central banks with valuable insights into spending patterns, liquidity needs, and overall economic activity. This data can enhance the ability of central banks to monitor economic conditions, forecast trends, and adjust monetary policy measures more dynamically.

Improved Financial Inclusion: CBDCs can promote financial inclusion by providing access to digital financial services for unbanked and underbanked populations. Greater financial inclusion can enhance the transmission of monetary policy, as a larger proportion of the population can be reached through digital channels. This inclusivity can support broader economic stability and growth.

Challenges for Monetary Policy with CBDCs

Disintermediation of Banks: One of the significant challenges posed by CBDCs is the potential disintermediation of commercial banks. If individuals and businesses prefer to hold CBDCs directly with the central bank rather than deposits with commercial banks, it could lead to a reduction in bank deposits. This disintermediation could impact banks' ability to lend and manage liquidity, potentially destabilizing the financial system.

Operational and Technological Risks: The implementation of CBDCs involves significant operational and technological risks. Ensuring the security, scalability, and reliability of CBDC systems is essential to prevent cyberattacks, operational failures, and other disruptions that could undermine confidence in the digital currency and monetary policy.

Regulatory and Legal Frameworks: The introduction of CBDCs requires the development of comprehensive regulatory and legal frameworks. These frameworks must address issues such as data privacy, cybersecurity, anti-money laundering (AML), counter-terrorism financing (CTF), and consumer protection. Establishing clear guidelines and ensuring regulatory compliance are critical to maintaining the integrity and stability of the financial system.

Monetary Sovereignty and International Coordination: The

widespread adoption of CBDCs could impact monetary sovereignty, particularly in countries with less stable currencies. If individuals and businesses prefer to hold foreign CBDCs over the domestic currency, it could lead to currency substitution and loss of control over domestic monetary policy. International coordination is necessary to address these risks and ensure that the global monetary system remains stable and coherent.

Managing Public Expectations and Trust: Building public trust and managing expectations are crucial for the successful implementation of CBDCs. Central banks must engage in transparent communication and education efforts to explain the benefits and risks of CBDCs, address concerns, and ensure that the public understands how to use digital currencies safely and effectively.

Case Studies: CBDCs and Monetary Policy

Several countries are exploring the use of CBDCs to enhance monetary policy, providing valuable insights into the opportunities and challenges associated with their implementation.

China's Digital Yuan: China's digital yuan, or Digital Currency Electronic Payment (DCEP), is one of the most advanced CBDC initiatives. The People's Bank of China (PBOC) has conducted extensive pilot programs to test the digital yuan's impact on monetary policy. These pilots have demonstrated the potential for the digital yuan to provide precise control over the money supply, improve the transmission of monetary policy, and enhance financial inclusion. However, the PBOC also faces challenges related to data privacy, cybersecurity, and regulatory compliance.

Sweden's e-Krona: Sweden's Riksbank is exploring the development of an e-Krona to complement cash and ensure access to central bank money in an increasingly digital economy. The e-Krona aims to enhance monetary policy by providing a secure and efficient means of payment. Pilot programs have shown that the e-Krona can improve the effectiveness of monetary policy measures, particularly in promoting financial inclusion and reducing the reliance on commercial banks. The Riksbank is addressing challenges related to technological infrastructure, regulatory frameworks, and public trust.

The Bahamas' Sand Dollar: The Central Bank of The Bahamas launched the Sand Dollar to promote financial inclusion and enhance the efficiency of monetary policy. The Sand Dollar allows for the direct transmission of monetary policy measures, such as stimulus payments, to citizens' digital wallets. This direct approach has improved the central bank's ability to support economic activity and stabilize the economy during times of crisis. The Central Bank of The Bahamas continues to address challenges related to digital literacy, cybersecurity, and regulatory compliance.

The integration of CBDCs into monetary policy offers significant opportunities to enhance the effectiveness and precision of economic interventions. However, the successful implementation of CBDCs requires careful consideration of the associated challenges, including the potential disintermediation of banks, operational and technological risks, regulatory and legal frameworks, and the need for international coordination.

Central banks must navigate these complexities to harness the full potential of CBDCs for monetary policy. Continued innovation, collaboration, and transparent communication with stakeholders are essential to building public trust and ensuring that CBDCs contribute to a stable and resilient financial system.

As more countries explore and adopt CBDCs, the insights gained from pilot projects and early implementations will provide valuable lessons for future developments. By addressing the challenges and leveraging the opportunities presented by CBDCs, central banks can enhance their ability to manage economic stability, support financial inclusion, and promote sustainable economic growth in the digital age.

6.5 Central Banks' Strategies for Stability

The introduction and implementation of Central Bank Digital Currencies (CBDCs) necessitate robust strategies to maintain financial stability and ensure smooth integration into the existing financial system. Central banks must develop comprehensive approaches that address the technological, operational, regulatory, and economic challenges associated with CBDCs. This section explores the strategies central banks can employ to ensure stability in the digital age.

Developing Robust Technological Infrastructure

Central banks must invest in and develop robust technological infrastructure to support the issuance, distribution, and management of CBDCs. This infrastructure should ensure scalability, security, and reliability to handle the volume and complexity of transactions associated with digital currencies.

Scalability: The CBDC platform must be capable of handling a large number of transactions simultaneously without degradation in performance. Central banks should collaborate with technology providers to build scalable systems that can accommodate future growth and increased usage.

Security: Ensuring the security of CBDC transactions is paramount to maintaining public trust and preventing cyber threats. Central banks must implement advanced encryption, authentication, and fraud detection measures to protect against cyberattacks and unauthorized access.

Reliability: The CBDC infrastructure must be highly reliable, with minimal downtime and robust disaster recovery mechanisms. Central banks should establish redundant systems and backup protocols to ensure continuous operation even in the face of technical failures or disruptions.

Establishing Clear Regulatory Frameworks

The introduction of CBDCs requires clear and comprehensive regulatory frameworks to govern their use and ensure compliance with existing financial regulations. Central banks must work closely with regulatory bodies to develop guidelines that address key issues such as anti-money laundering (AML), counter-terrorism financing (CTF), data privacy, and consumer protection.

Anti-Money Laundering (AML) and Counter-Terrorism Financing (CTF): CBDCs must be designed to comply with AML and CTF regulations, with built-in mechanisms for monitoring and reporting suspicious activities. Central banks should establish protocols for identifying and addressing potential risks associated with illicit financial activities.

Data Privacy: Protecting the privacy of users' financial data is essential to maintaining public trust in CBDCs. Central banks must develop data privacy policies that balance the need for transparency with the protection of individual privacy. This includes implementing data anonymization techniques and ensuring compliance with relevant data protection regulations.

Consumer Protection: Ensuring the protection of consumers is critical to the success of CBDCs. Central banks should establish guidelines for consumer rights, dispute resolution, and fraud prevention. This includes providing clear information about the risks and benefits of using CBDCs and offering support services for users.

Promoting Financial Inclusion

One of the key benefits of CBDCs is their potential to enhance financial inclusion. Central banks must develop strategies to ensure that CBDCs are accessible and beneficial to all segments of the population, particularly underserved and unbanked individuals.

Accessibility: CBDCs should be designed to be user-friendly and accessible to individuals with varying levels of digital literacy. This includes developing mobile applications with intuitive interfaces, providing support for multiple languages, and offering offline transaction capabilities for areas with limited internet access.

Education and Outreach: Central banks should implement educational campaigns to inform the public about the benefits and usage of CBDCs. These campaigns should target underserved communities and provide training on digital financial literacy, ensuring that individuals understand how to use CBDCs safely and effectively.

Collaborating with Financial Institutions

Collaboration with financial institutions is essential for the successful implementation of CBDCs. Central banks must work closely with commercial banks, payment service providers, and fintech companies to ensure seamless integration and broad adoption of CBDCs.

Integration with Existing Systems: CBDCs should be designed to integrate seamlessly with existing financial systems and payment platforms. Central banks should collaborate with financial institutions to develop interoperability standards and ensure that CBDCs can be used alongside traditional forms of money.

Partnerships with Fintech Companies: Fintech companies can play a crucial role in the development and deployment of CBDC-related services. Central banks should establish partnerships with fintech firms to leverage their expertise in technology and innovation, enhancing the functionality and usability of CBDCs.

Addressing Economic and Monetary Policy Implications

The introduction of CBDCs has significant implications for economic and monetary policy. Central banks must carefully consider these implications and develop strategies to manage the potential impacts on financial stability, monetary policy transmission, and economic activity.

Managing Financial Stability Risks: Central banks should conduct thorough risk assessments to identify potential threats to financial stability associated with CBDCs. This includes addressing the risk of bank disintermediation, ensuring adequate liquidity in the financial system, and developing contingency plans for crisis situations.

Enhancing Monetary Policy Transmission: CBDCs offer new tools for implementing monetary policy, such as direct distribution of stimulus payments and the ability to impose negative interest rates. Central banks should explore these opportunities and develop strategies to enhance the transmission and effectiveness of monetary policy in the digital age.

Monitoring Economic Activity: The data generated by CBDC transactions can provide valuable insights into economic activity and consumer behavior. Central banks should leverage this data to improve economic forecasting, identify emerging trends, and adjust policy measures as needed to support economic stability and growth.

Building Public Trust and Confidence

The success of CBDCs depends on building public trust and confidence in the digital currency. Central banks must engage in transparent communication and actively address public concerns to ensure broad acceptance and adoption of CBDCs.

Transparent Communication: Central banks should provide clear and transparent information about the design, benefits, and risks of CBDCs. This includes publishing detailed reports, conducting public consultations, and engaging with stakeholders to address their concerns and gather feedback.

Addressing Public Concerns: Common concerns about CBDCs include data privacy, security, and the potential for misuse. Central banks must address these concerns through robust policy measures, technological safeguards, and ongoing public engagement. Providing reassurances about the safety and security of CBDCs is essential for building public trust.

Continuous Improvement and Innovation

The development and implementation of CBDCs are ongoing processes that require continuous improvement and innovation. Central banks must remain adaptable and open to new technologies and approaches to ensure the long-term success and stability of CBDCs.

Adapting to Technological Advances: The financial technology landscape is constantly evolving, with new developments in blockchain, encryption, and digital payments. Central banks should stay informed about these advances and be prepared to incorporate new technologies into the CBDC infrastructure to enhance functionality and security.

Ongoing Research and Development: Central banks should invest in ongoing research and development to explore new use cases for CBDCs, address emerging challenges, and improve the overall effectiveness of digital currencies. This includes collaborating with academic institutions, industry experts, and other central banks to share knowledge and best practices.

The successful implementation of CBDCs requires comprehensive strategies that address technological, regulatory, economic, and public trust considerations. Central banks must develop robust technological infrastructure, establish clear regulatory frameworks, promote financial inclusion, collaborate with financial institutions, manage economic implications, build public trust, and continuously innovate to ensure the stability and effectiveness of CBDCs in the digital age. By adopting these strategies, central banks can harness the full potential of CBDCs to enhance financial stability, support economic growth, and promote a more inclusive and resilient financial system.

The introduction and proliferation of Central Bank Digital Currencies (CBDCs) represent a transformative shift in the landscape of global finance, necessitating a reevaluation of the roles and responsibilities of constitutional and duly constituted authorities. These entities, which include central banks, regulatory bodies, legislative assemblies, and executive branches, play a critical role in ensuring the stability, security, and integrity of the financial system. The successful implementation and management of CBDCs require these authorities to adapt to new technological realities, develop comprehensive regulatory frameworks, and maintain the public's trust in the evolving digital economy.

Central banks, as the issuers and regulators of CBDCs, are at the forefront of this transformation. They must not only develop the technological infrastructure necessary for CBDC issuance and management but also ensure that these digital currencies are integrated seamlessly into the existing financial system. This involves designing CBDCs that are secure, scalable, and resilient to cyber threats while also being user-friendly and accessible to the general population. Central banks must also conduct extensive research and pilot programs to test the functionality and impact of CBDCs, gathering data and insights that can inform policy decisions and operational strategies.

Regulatory bodies play an essential role in establishing the legal and regulatory frameworks that govern the use of CBDCs. These frameworks must address a wide range of issues, including anti-money laundering (AML) and counter-terrorism financing (CTF) measures, data privacy and protection, consumer rights, and the interoperability of CBDCs with other digital payment systems. Regulatory authorities must work closely with central banks to ensure that these regulations are robust and comprehensive, providing clear guidelines for financial institutions and consumers. Additionally, regulators must continuously monitor the CBDC ecosystem for compliance and potential risks, implementing corrective measures as needed to maintain the integrity of the financial system.

Legislative assemblies are responsible for enacting the laws that underpin the regulatory frameworks for CBDCs. Lawmakers must engage in informed debates and consultations to understand the implications of digital currencies and ensure that the legal framework is conducive to innovation while protecting the public interest. This includes addressing issues such as the legal status of CBDCs, the rights and obligations of users, and the jurisdictional challenges that arise from cross-border digital transactions. Legislators must also consider the broader economic and social impacts of CBDCs, such as their potential to enhance financial inclusion and reduce transaction costs, and incorporate these considerations into the legal framework.

The executive branch of government, including ministries of finance and economic development, plays a pivotal role in coordinating the national strategy for CBDC implementation. This involves aligning the efforts of central banks, regulatory bodies, and legislative assemblies to create a cohesive and effective policy environment. The executive branch must also engage with international counterparts and organizations to address the global dimensions of CBDC adoption, including standards for cross-border transactions and mechanisms for international cooperation. Furthermore, government agencies must implement public education campaigns to inform citizens about the benefits and risks of CBDCs, promoting widespread understanding and acceptance of digital currencies.

Public trust is a fundamental pillar of the successful adoption of CBDCs. Constitutional and duly constituted authorities must prioritize building and maintaining this trust through transparency, accountability, and effective communication. Central banks and regulatory bodies must provide clear and accessible information about the design, functionality, and security of CBDCs, addressing public concerns and dispelling misconceptions. Regular updates on the progress of CBDC projects, as well as opportunities for public consultation and feedback, can enhance transparency and foster a sense of ownership and confidence among citizens.

Data privacy and protection are critical considerations in the design and implementation of CBDCs. Authorities must ensure that the use of digital currencies does not compromise individuals' privacy rights or expose them to undue risks. This involves implementing robust data encryption and security measures, as well as establishing clear policies for data access, usage, and retention. Regulatory frameworks must also include provisions for auditing and oversight to ensure compliance with data protection standards. By safeguarding data privacy, authorities can build public trust in CBDCs and encourage their adoption.

Interoperability with existing financial systems and other digital payment platforms is essential for the seamless integration of CBDCs. Central banks and regulatory bodies must work with financial institutions and technology providers to develop standards and protocols that enable CBDCs to function alongside traditional currencies and payment systems. This includes addressing technical challenges related to transaction processing, settlement, and cross-border payments. Ensuring interoperability will enhance the usability and convenience of CBDCs, making them a viable and attractive option for consumers and businesses.

The potential impact of CBDCs on monetary policy and financial stability requires careful consideration and strategic planning by central banks and government authorities. CBDCs offer new tools for implementing monetary policy, such as the ability to apply negative interest rates directly to digital currency holdings or to distribute stimulus payments efficiently. However, they also pose risks, such as the possibility of disintermediation of commercial banks or increased volatility in financial markets. Authorities must conduct thorough analyses and simulations to understand these impacts and develop strategies to mitigate risks while maximizing the benefits of CBDCs for economic management.

International cooperation and coordination are crucial for addressing the global implications of CBDCs. As digital currencies transcend national borders, authorities must work together to establish common standards, share best practices, and develop mechanisms for regulatory harmonization. This cooperation can help prevent regulatory arbitrage, where entities exploit differences in national regulations to engage in risky or illicit activities. International organizations, such as the International Monetary Fund (IMF) and the Bank for International Settlements (BIS), can play a pivotal role in facilitating dialogue and cooperation among countries, providing a platform for collaboration and knowledge exchange.

Educational and training programs for government officials, financial professionals, and the general public are essential for the successful implementation and management of CBDCs. Authorities must invest in developing the skills and knowledge needed to navigate the complexities of digital currencies. This includes training for central bank staff on the technical and operational aspects of CBDCs, as well as educational initiatives for financial institutions on compliance and best practices.

Public education campaigns can help demystify CBDCs and encourage informed and responsible use by citizens.

The transition to a digital currency system requires a phased and adaptive approach. Authorities must adopt a flexible strategy that allows for iterative testing, feedback, and adjustment. Pilot programs and controlled rollouts can provide valuable insights into the practical challenges and opportunities of CBDCs, enabling authorities to refine their approaches before full-scale implementation. Continuous monitoring and evaluation of CBDC projects are essential to ensure that they meet their objectives and adapt to evolving technological and economic conditions.

The successful implementation and management of CBDCs depend on the coordinated efforts of constitutional and duly constituted authorities. Central banks, regulatory bodies, legislative assemblies, and executive branches must work together to develop robust technological infrastructure, establish clear regulatory frameworks, promote financial inclusion, and build public trust. By addressing the challenges and leveraging the opportunities presented by CBDCs, these authorities can ensure the stability, security, and integrity of the financial system in the digital age. Through transparency, accountability, and international cooperation, they can foster a resilient and inclusive digital economy that benefits all stakeholders.

CHAPTER 7: REGULATORY FRAMEWORKS FOR CBDCS

7.1 Current Financial Regulations and Their Applicability to CBDCs

The introduction of Central Bank Digital Currencies (CBDCs) necessitates a thorough examination of existing financial regulations and their applicability to this new form of digital money. Traditional financial regulations, designed for a world of physical currency and traditional banking, must be reassessed and potentially adapted to ensure they are fit for purpose in a digital age. This section explores the current financial regulations that impact CBDCs and discusses how these regulations may need to evolve to accommodate the unique characteristics and challenges of digital currencies.

Anti-Money Laundering (AML) and Counter-Terrorism Financing (CTF)

One of the primary concerns with the introduction of CBDCs is ensuring that they do not facilitate money laundering or terrorism financing. Existing AML and CTF regulations are designed to detect and prevent illicit financial activities by requiring financial institutions to monitor transactions, verify customer identities, and report suspicious activities to authorities. These regulations must be adapted to cover CBDC transactions effectively.

CBDCs offer enhanced transparency and traceability compared to cash, which can make it easier to track the flow of funds and identify suspicious activities. However, the digital nature of CBDCs also presents new challenges, such as the potential for sophisticated cybercrimes and the need to balance transparency with data privacy. Regulators must develop frameworks that leverage the transparency of CBDCs while implementing robust security measures to protect against illicit activities.

Data Privacy and Protection

Data privacy is a critical consideration in the design and implementation of CBDCs. Traditional financial regulations include provisions to protect the privacy of individuals' financial data, such as the General Data Protection Regulation (GDPR) in the European Union and the California Consumer Privacy Act (CCPA) in the United States. These regulations must be reassessed to ensure they adequately address the unique data privacy issues associated with CBDCs.

CBDCs generate vast amounts of transaction data that can provide valuable insights into economic activity and consumer behavior. However, this data must be handled with care to protect individuals' privacy rights. Regulators must establish clear guidelines for data collection, storage, access, and usage. This includes implementing data anonymization techniques, ensuring that only authorized entities have access to sensitive information, and providing individuals with control over their personal data.

Consumer Protection

Ensuring the protection of consumers is essential for

building trust in CBDCs. Existing consumer protection regulations are designed to safeguard individuals from fraud, ensure transparency in financial transactions, and provide mechanisms for dispute resolution. These regulations must be adapted to address the specific risks and challenges associated with CBDCs.

Regulators must establish clear guidelines for consumer rights and protections in the context of CBDCs. This includes providing transparent information about the risks and benefits of using digital currencies, implementing safeguards against fraud and cyber threats, and ensuring that consumers have access to effective mechanisms for resolving disputes. Additionally, regulators must consider the potential impact of CBDCs on vulnerable populations and ensure that protections are in place to prevent exploitation.

Financial Stability and Systemic Risk

The introduction of CBDCs has significant implications for financial stability and systemic risk. Existing regulations designed to maintain financial stability, such as capital requirements for banks and liquidity coverage ratios, must be reassessed to ensure they are effective in a world with digital currencies.

CBDCs can provide central banks with new tools for managing liquidity and implementing monetary policy. However, they also pose risks, such as the potential for bank disintermediation and increased volatility in financial markets. Regulators must develop frameworks that address these risks and ensure that CBDCs contribute to, rather than undermine, financial stability. This includes establishing protocols for managing systemic risks, conducting stress tests and simulations, and developing contingency plans for crisis situations.

Interoperability and International Coordination

CBDCs have the potential to facilitate cross-border transactions and enhance global financial integration. However, achieving these benefits requires interoperability between different CBDC systems and coordination between national regulatory frameworks. Existing regulations governing cross-border payments, foreign exchange transactions, and international financial flows must be adapted to address the unique challenges of CBDCs.

Regulators must work together to develop common standards and protocols for CBDC interoperability. This includes establishing guidelines for cross-border data sharing, ensuring compliance with international AML and CTF regulations, and developing mechanisms for regulatory harmonization. International organizations, such as the International Monetary Fund (IMF) and the Bank for International Settlements (BIS), can play a crucial role in facilitating dialogue and cooperation between countries.

Legal Frameworks and Central Bank Mandates

The legal frameworks governing the issuance and use of money must be updated to reflect the introduction of CBDCs. This includes clarifying the legal status of CBDCs, defining the rights and obligations of users, and ensuring that central banks have the necessary mandates to issue and regulate digital currencies.

Regulators must ensure that the legal frameworks for CBDCs are consistent with broader monetary and financial policies. This includes addressing issues related to monetary sovereignty, currency competition, and the role of central banks in the digital economy. Clear legal frameworks are essential for providing certainty and stability in the use of CBDCs, supporting their widespread adoption, and ensuring that they contribute to the overall objectives of monetary policy and financial regulation.

Technological and Operational Standards

The successful implementation of CBDCs requires the development of robust technological and operational standards. These standards must address issues related to cybersecurity, system resilience, and transaction processing. Existing regulations governing the operation of payment systems and financial infrastructure must be adapted to ensure they are fit for the digital age.

Regulators must work with technology providers and financial institutions to develop standards that ensure the security and reliability of CBDC systems. This includes establishing protocols for encryption, authentication, and fraud detection, as well as developing guidelines for system maintenance, upgrades, and incident response. Ensuring that CBDC systems are resilient to cyber threats and operational failures is critical for maintaining public trust and ensuring the stability of the financial system.

Public Engagement and Transparency

Public engagement and transparency are essential for building trust in CBDCs and ensuring their successful adoption. Regulators must engage with stakeholders, including the public, financial institutions, and policymakers, to gather feedback and address concerns. Transparent communication about the design, functionality, and security of CBDCs is crucial for fostering public confidence.

Regulators should conduct public consultations and provide opportunities for stakeholders to participate in the development of regulatory frameworks for CBDCs. This includes publishing detailed reports, holding public hearings, and engaging with community organizations. Transparent and inclusive regulatory processes can help build broad-based support for CBDCs and ensure that their implementation reflects the needs and concerns of all stakeholders.

The introduction of CBDCs represents a significant

shift in the landscape of global finance, requiring a comprehensive reevaluation of existing financial regulations and their applicability to digital currencies. Ensuring the effective regulation of CBDCs requires collaboration between central banks, regulatory bodies, legislative assemblies, and international organizations. By developing clear and robust regulatory frameworks, addressing key issues such as AML, data privacy, consumer protection, financial stability, interoperability, and public trust, authorities can ensure that CBDCs contribute to a stable, secure, and inclusive financial system in the digital age. The successful regulation of CBDCs will require continuous innovation, adaptation, and engagement with stakeholders, reflecting the dynamic nature of the evolving digital economy.

Regulating CBDCs also involves addressing the potential for economic disruption. As digital currencies could fundamentally change the way monetary transactions are conducted, there is a need for carefully crafted economic policies that consider both short-term impacts and long-term implications. Policymakers must analyze how CBDCs could affect different sectors of the economy, including small businesses, large corporations, and the informal sector, and develop strategies to mitigate any negative consequences.

Macro-Economic Considerations

The macro-economic implications of CBDCs are significant. By providing central banks with a new tool for monetary policy execution, CBDCs can influence inflation, interest rates, and overall economic growth. These currencies offer the potential for more direct mechanisms of implementing policy changes, such as altering interest rates on digital wallets to encourage spending or saving. However, this also raises concerns about the central bank's role in the economy and the potential for increased government oversight of citizens' financial activities. Therefore, it is crucial for regulatory frameworks to include strict guidelines on how these powerful tools are used, ensuring that monetary policy remains transparent and predictable.

Balancing Innovation and Regulation

While regulation is essential for ensuring stability and security, it must also be balanced with the need for innovation. Over-regulation could stifle the development and adoption of CBDCs, hindering their potential benefits. To encourage innovation, regulators can adopt a phased approach, starting with pilot programs and controlled rollouts that allow for iterative learning and adjustment before full-scale implementation. These programs can help identify potential problems in a controlled environment, allowing regulators to develop more informed and effective policies.

Moreover, the feedback from these pilots can inform ongoing legislative processes, ensuring that laws remain adaptive and responsive to new developments. This approach not only protects against unforeseen consequences but also fosters a regulatory environment that supports technological advancement and economic growth.

International Standards and Cooperation

Given the global nature of finance, international cooperation is essential in the regulation of CBDCs. Different countries may have varying approaches to digital currency, and without a coordinated effort, this could lead to a fragmented and inefficient global financial system. International standards can help ensure interoperability between different CBDC systems, facilitating cross-border transactions and reducing the risk of currency fragmentation.

Organizations such as the International Monetary Fund (IMF), the World Bank, and the Bank for International Settlements (BIS) can play a pivotal role in fostering international dialogue and coordination. These bodies can help harmonize regulatory approaches, ensuring that CBDCs support global trade and economic stability. By sharing data, insights, and best practices, countries can develop policies that not only benefit their economies but also contribute to a more stable and interconnected global financial system.

Risk Management and Contingency Planning

Effective risk management is critical in the regulation of CBDCs. Central banks and financial regulators need to establish comprehensive risk assessment and management frameworks that address potential cybersecurity risks, operational failures, and economic impacts. This involves continuous monitoring of the CBDC ecosystem, regular stress testing of the infrastructure, and the development of contingency plans to address potential crises.

Risk management strategies should be integrated into the broader national security framework, as the implications of a failure in a CBDC system could extend beyond financial losses to broader economic and social consequences. Collaboration between financial authorities, cybersecurity agencies, and private sector stakeholders is vital to ensure a robust defense against threats.

Education and Consumer Awareness

Finally, educating consumers about the features, benefits, and risks of CBDCs is essential for their successful adoption. Regulatory frameworks should mandate the provision of clear, accessible information that helps users make informed decisions about using digital currencies. This includes understanding the protections available to them, the implications of their privacy choices, and how to securely manage digital wallets.

Consumer education campaigns can be supported by schools, non-profits, and private sector partners, ensuring that messages reach a wide audience and contribute to a well-informed public that can leverage CBDCs to enhance their financial well-being and economic opportunities.

As CBDCs redefine the landscape of monetary systems, the regulatory frameworks governing them must be dynamic, comprehensive, and forward-looking. These frameworks should not only address the immediate technical and security concerns but also consider broader economic, social, and international implications. By fostering an environment that balances regulation with innovation, promotes international cooperation, manages risks effectively, and prioritizes consumer education, policymakers can ensure that CBDCs contribute to a stable, secure, and prosperous financial future.

7.2 Proposing New Regulatory Frameworks for CBDCs

As the global financial landscape evolves with the advent of Central Bank Digital Currencies (CBDCs), the necessity for novel regulatory frameworks becomes apparent. These frameworks must be designed not only to govern the issuance and operation of CBDCs but also to ensure their safe integration into the broader financial system. This involves addressing a spectrum of concerns from systemic risks to individual privacy, while also fostering innovation and maintaining the stability of the financial system.

FUNDAMENTAL PRINCIPLES OF CBDC REGULATION

The development of regulatory frameworks for CBDCs should be guided by a set of fundamental principles:

1. Security and Stability: At the core, the regulatory framework must ensure the security and stability of CBDC transactions. This includes robust measures against cyber threats, fraud, and operational risks, ensuring that CBDC systems are resilient and reliable.

2. Privacy and Transparency: Regulations should balance the need for transparency in financial transactions to prevent illicit activities with the imperative to protect individual privacy. This requires clear rules on data collection, processing, and sharing that align with global data protection standards.

3. Interoperability and Inclusiveness: To facilitate widespread adoption and utility, CBDCs should be interoperable with existing financial systems and other digital currencies. Additionally, the regulatory framework should ensure that CBDC systems are inclusive and accessible to all segments of the population, including those in rural or underserved areas.

4. Innovation and Flexibility: The regulatory approach should encourage innovation by providing a clear, flexible framework that can adapt to technological advancements and evolving market conditions. This includes supporting experimentation and pilot testing through regulatory sandboxes or similar initiatives.

PROPOSED REGULATORY DOMAINS

Given these guiding principles, the new regulatory frameworks for CBDCs can be organized into several key domains:

1. Issuance and Distribution

Regulations concerning the issuance and distribution of CBDCs need to ensure that these processes are carried out by the central bank or designated financial institutions under strict guidelines. This includes:

- Setting standards for the technological infrastructure used in the issuance and distribution of CBDCs.
- Establishing criteria for determining eligibility to access CBDCs.
- Defining the operational procedures for issuing, distributing, and redeeming CBDCs.

2. Transaction Monitoring and Reporting

To combat financial crimes such as money laundering and terrorism financing, regulators must implement transaction monitoring and reporting requirements for CBDCs similar to those for traditional banking instruments. This includes:

- Mandating that all CBDC transactions are monitored for suspicious activity.
- Requiring financial institutions to report large transactions and suspicious activities to relevant authorities.
- Utilizing advanced analytics and machine learning to enhance the effectiveness of monitoring systems.

3. Consumer Protection

Consumer protection regulations should address the specific risks associated with digital currencies. These include:

- Ensuring that consumers are adequately informed about the risks and benefits of using CBDCs.
- Establishing mechanisms for dispute resolution and redress in cases of fraud, error, or other issues.
- Implementing safeguards against technological failures, ensuring that users' assets are protected.

4. Technological Standards

Given the critical role of technology in the operation of CBDCs, regulatory frameworks must set high standards for software and hardware involved in CBDC systems. This includes:

- Defining security protocols for CBDC wallets and other interfaces.
- Setting benchmarks for system uptime and resilience.
- Mandating regular audits and stress tests of CBDC infrastructures.

5. Cross-Border Considerations

With the global nature of financial transactions, it is essential that CBDC regulations address cross-border issues, including:

- Establishing guidelines for international transactions using CBDCs, including conversion rates and procedures.
- Coordinating with international regulatory bodies to ensure compliance across jurisdictions.
- Developing systems to monitor and manage cross-border financial flows to prevent evasion of capital controls and other regulatory measures.

6. Legal and Compliance

Finally, legal and compliance aspects must be thoroughly addressed in the regulatory frameworks for CBDCs, including:

- Defining the legal tender status of CBDCs.
- Updating tax laws and regulations to account for CBDC transactions.
- Ensuring that CBDC regulations comply with existing financial laws and international agreements.

IMPLEMENTATION STRATEGIES

Implementing these regulatory frameworks requires a phased approach, starting with extensive stakeholder consultations to ensure that the regulations are comprehensive and do not stifle innovation. Pilot programs should be initiated to test the regulatory frameworks in controlled environments, allowing for adjustments based on empirical evidence and feedback.

The successful regulation of CBDCs demands a thoughtful and balanced approach that addresses the complex challenges posed by digital currencies. By developing regulatory frameworks that uphold security, encourage innovation, ensure privacy, and promote inclusivity, central banks and regulators can pave the way for CBDCs to contribute positively to the global financial system. The transition to digital currencies represents a significant evolution in monetary policy and financial regulation, and as such, requires diligent planning, robust stakeholder engagement, and continual adaptation to emerging challenges and opportunities.

7.3 Case Studies: Successful Regulation Models

In the evolving landscape of Central Bank Digital Currencies (CBDCs), several countries have emerged as pioneers, developing regulatory frameworks that may serve as blueprints for others. This section examines case studies from various jurisdictions that have successfully implemented CBDCs, focusing on their regulatory approaches, the challenges they faced, and the solutions they employed. These examples provide valuable insights into the complexity of regulating digital currencies and highlight effective strategies for ensuring their safe and beneficial use.

CASE STUDY 1: THE BAHAMAS' SAND DOLLAR

The Bahamas was one of the first countries to fully deploy a CBDC, the Sand Dollar, aimed at enhancing financial inclusion and resilience across its archipelago. The regulatory approach taken by The Central Bank of The Bahamas focused on creating an inclusive framework that facilitated access to digital payments across its many islands.

Regulatory Focus:
- Inclusivity and Accessibility: Regulations were crafted to ensure that the Sand Dollar could be easily accessed by all residents, including those on less populated islands without robust banking infrastructure.
- Privacy and Security: The Central Bank implemented stringent security measures to protect users' data while also ensuring that the system adhered to international standards for data protection and privacy.

- Interoperability: The Sand Dollar was designed to be fully interoperable with existing financial systems, allowing seamless transactions between digital and fiat currencies.

Challenges and Solutions:
- The primary challenge was building an infrastructure that could operate reliably across remote and often less technologically developed areas. The solution involved leveraging mobile technology and developing offline transaction capabilities, ensuring that transactions could be processed even without continuous internet access.
- Ensuring user trust was another challenge, addressed through extensive public education campaigns and transparent communication about the safety and benefits of the Sand Dollar.

CASE STUDY 2: CHINA'S DIGITAL YUAN

China's digital yuan, also known as the e-CNY, represents one of the most significant trials in CBDCs globally. The People's Bank of China (PBoC) aims to increase the efficiency of retail payments domestically and eventually enhance yuan's use in international transactions.

Regulatory Focus:
- Control and Monitoring: The PBoC maintained strict control over the issuance and circulation of the digital yuan, ensuring it complemented existing monetary policies and financial systems.
- Consumer Protection: Robust mechanisms were put in place to protect consumers' rights, ensuring transparency in transactions and the security of funds.
- Anti-Money Laundering (AML): Regulations were enhanced to prevent money laundering and ensure that the digital yuan could not be used for illegal activities.

Challenges and Solutions:
- Balancing privacy with surveillance was a major challenge, managed by anonymizing transaction data while retaining

the necessary information for legal compliance and financial monitoring.
- The potential for disintermediation of commercial banks was mitigated by involving them in the digital yuan ecosystem, allowing them to issue and manage digital wallets.

CASE STUDY 3: SWEDEN'S E-KRONA

Sweden has been exploring the e-Krona due to the declining use of cash in the country. The Riksbank focused on ensuring that the e-Krona complemented existing payment systems and did not replace cash but provided a digital alternative.

Regulatory Focus:
- Financial Stability: The framework ensured that the introduction of the e-Krona did not disrupt the existing financial system but rather supported financial stability.
- Innovation Encouragement: The Riksbank encouraged innovation in the digital payment space by allowing private sector participation in the e-Krona ecosystem.
- User Education: Significant resources were devoted to educating the public on the use of the e-Krona, addressing concerns related to digital finance, and promoting digital literacy.

Challenges and Solutions:
- Addressing the digital divide was critical, particularly in ensuring that older populations and those less familiar with digital technology could access and use the e-Krona. Solutions included user-friendly design, widespread public education programs, and easy access through various technologies.
- Maintaining transaction integrity and preventing cyber threats were addressed through state-of-the-art cybersecurity measures and continuous monitoring of the e-Krona's infrastructure.

CASE STUDY 4: EASTERN CARIBBEAN CURRENCY UNION'S DCASH

The Eastern Caribbean Central Bank (ECCB) launched DCash,

a digital version of the Eastern Caribbean dollar, aimed at improving financial inclusion and reducing transaction costs across multiple island nations.

Regulatory Focus:
- Cross-Border Efficiency: Regulations facilitated efficient cross-border transactions within the currency union, promoting economic integration.
- Resilience and Redundancy: The ECCB implemented robust systems to ensure the resilience of the DCash platform, with multiple layers of redundancy to handle failures and ensure continuity of operations.

Challenges and Solutions:
- One challenge was the logistical complexity of deploying a unified digital currency across different jurisdictions with varying legal and financial environments. The ECCB addressed this by closely collaborating with financial institutions and governments of member countries to align regulations and infrastructure.
- Ensuring robust participation across the region involved extensive promotional campaigns and partnerships with local financial entities to foster trust and encourage adoption.

These case studies reveal that while the path to regulating CBDCs can be complex and fraught with challenges, thorough planning, stakeholder engagement, and adaptive regulatory frameworks can lead to successful implementations. Each jurisdiction's approach offers unique lessons that can inform other central banks and regulatory bodies as they embark on their own CBDC initiatives.

CASE STUDY 5: SINGAPORE'S PROJECT UBIN

Singapore has been at the forefront of exploring blockchain and digital currencies through Project Ubin, which is a multi-phase initiative to explore the use of blockchain and distributed ledger technology for clearing and settlement of payments and securities. The Monetary Authority of Singapore (MAS) has been collaborating with private sector finance firms to develop and test new uses of this technology.

Regulatory Focus:
- Innovation-friendly Environment: MAS has created a regulatory environment that encourages innovation while ensuring system security and integrity. This includes the creation of a regulatory sandbox that allows fintech startups and other financial institutions to test new blockchain technologies and business models in a controlled environment.
- Comprehensive Risk Management: The framework emphasizes the management of risks associated with digital transactions, including cyber security risks, operational risks, and counterparty risks.
- Global Collaboration: MAS has actively sought international partnerships to ensure that its digital currency initiatives align with global standards and can interface seamlessly with other national digital currencies.

Challenges and Solutions:
- Ensuring interoperability between different blockchain platforms was a challenge, addressed by standardizing APIs and promoting the use of common frameworks and protocols.
- MAS also faced the challenge of ensuring the privacy of transactions while maintaining the ability to perform necessary regulatory oversight and prevent illicit financial activities. This was managed by using privacy-preserving technologies that still allowed for selective transparency.

CASE STUDY 6: CANADA'S PROJECT JASPER

The Bank of Canada's exploration of a digital currency through Project Jasper has provided significant insights into how a digital currency could be integrated into the national economy. Project Jasper focuses on the use of a digital currency for wholesale transactions rather than retail transactions, exploring potential efficiencies in the settlement of transactions.

Regulatory Focus:
- Systemic Stability: Ensuring that the introduction of a digital currency does not undermine the stability of the financial system, with specific attention to liquidity risks.
- Collaborative Development: Working in partnership with major commercial banks and financial institutions to ensure that the new technology integrates well with existing financial infrastructure.
- Legal Clarity: Developing clear legal frameworks that define the status of digital records, digital signatures, and their acceptability in financial transactions.

Challenges and Solutions:
- One of the primary challenges was the integration of digital currency technology into the existing financial system without disrupting ongoing operations. This was approached by phased testing and implementation, allowing for gradual integration.
- Another challenge was maintaining the efficiency and security of high-value transfers. Project Jasper utilized cutting-edge cryptographic techniques, including the use of distributed ledgers that ensure both transparency and security of transactions.

CASE STUDY 7: EUROPEAN CENTRAL BANK'S DIGITAL EURO

The European Central Bank (ECB) has been actively exploring the concept of a digital euro, aimed at complementing cash and ensuring that the public remains able to use central bank money even as the use of physical cash declines. The digital euro project considers both retail and wholesale uses of digital currency.

Regulatory Focus:
- Consumer Acceptance and Trust: The ECB places a strong emphasis on building consumer trust and acceptance, ensuring that digital euro solutions are secure, easy to use, and offer clear benefits over other forms of payment.

- Financial Inclusion: Ensuring the digital euro supports broader goals of financial inclusion by being accessible to all citizens, including those without regular access to digital technology.
- Monetary Sovereignty: Safeguarding the monetary sovereignty of eurozone nations by providing an official digital currency as an alternative to other digital payment solutions and cryptocurrencies.

Challenges and Solutions:
- The ECB faces the challenge of designing a system that can support a vast range of transactions across diverse economic regions. This involves developing advanced technological solutions that ensure scalability, resilience, and security.
- Another significant challenge is the legal integration of the digital euro into the existing financial laws and regulations of various member states. The ECB has been working closely with EU institutions to create a harmonized regulatory framework that supports the digital euro's deployment.

These case studies illuminate the multifaceted challenges and diverse strategies central banks across the globe employ as they navigate the introduction and regulation of CBDCs. The examples demonstrate the importance of adaptive regulatory frameworks, the potential for fostering innovation while ensuring stability and security, and the necessity for international collaboration in the increasingly interconnected global financial landscape.

7.4 Ensuring Compliance in a Digital Financial World

As the financial world transitions more towards digital operations, with Central Bank Digital Currencies (CBDCs) becoming a significant component, ensuring compliance poses unique challenges and requires innovative approaches. Regulatory bodies and financial institutions must adapt to these changes, ensuring that digital financial systems remain secure, transparent, and in accordance with established laws and standards. This section explores how compliance can be ensured in this evolving digital financial landscape.

REVISING REGULATORY FRAMEWORKS

The introduction of CBDCs necessitates a reevaluation and revision of existing regulatory frameworks to address the new dynamics introduced by digital currencies. Traditional financial regulations were designed for a world dominated by physical cash and conventional banking practices. As such, they may not fully address the risks or exploit the opportunities presented by digital financial systems.

1. Anti-Money Laundering (AML) and Counter-Terrorism Financing (CTF): Regulations need to be updated to account for the digital nature of CBDCs, which might simplify some aspects of monitoring but could also introduce new ways to obscure illicit fund flows. Enhanced digital tracking capabilities can be leveraged to improve surveillance and reporting systems.

2. Consumer Protection Laws: These laws must be expanded to ensure that users 'rights are protected in digital transactions. This includes clear guidelines on the recourse available to consumers in cases of fraud, errors, or disputes in digital transactions.

3. Data Protection and Privacy: With the increased digitization of financial information, ensuring the privacy and security of personal data becomes paramount. Regulations such as the GDPR in the European Union provide a framework that might be adapted to include specifics for the handling of financial data through CBDCs.

LEVERAGING TECHNOLOGY FOR COMPLIANCE

Technology not only presents challenges but also offers solutions for ensuring compliance. Blockchain and other distributed ledger technologies (DLT) that might underpin CBDCs provide inherent advantages such as traceability and transparency which can be leveraged to enhance compliance mechanisms.

1. Smart Contracts: These can automate compliance by embedding regulatory requirements into the CBDC transactions themselves. For example, smart contracts could automatically enforce limits on the amounts that can be transacted, or ensure that only authorized transactions occur between approved parties.

2. Enhanced Due Diligence Tools: Machine learning and artificial intelligence can analyze transaction patterns to identify unusual activities that may warrant further investigation. These tools can help in proactively monitoring and managing compliance risks in real-time.

INTERNATIONAL COOPERATION AND STANDARDS

The global nature of the financial system, coupled with the borderless characteristics of CBDCs, calls for international cooperation in developing compliance standards. This cooperation is crucial to prevent regulatory arbitrage, where parties could seek to exploit differences between regulatory regimes.

1. Harmonizing Regulatory Standards: International bodies like the Financial Action Task Force (FATF) and the International Monetary Fund (IMF) can play crucial roles in establishing global standards for CBDC operations. These standards can help ensure a level playing field and simplify compliance for international transactions.

2. Cross-border Collaborations: Agreements between countries can facilitate smoother cross-border transactions in CBDCs while ensuring that these transactions remain compliant with international laws and regulations. These agreements can also stipulate shared protocols for dealing with international

financial crimes.

TRAINING AND EDUCATION

Ensuring compliance in a digital financial world also requires a focus on human factors, particularly training and education for both regulators and the regulated entities.

1. Regulator Training: Regulators need to be well-versed in the new technologies and understand the complexities of digital currencies. Ongoing training programs can help maintain a high level of expertise among those tasked with monitoring and ensuring compliance.

2. Industry Education: Financial institutions and other parties involved in the issuance and management of CBDCs must understand their regulatory obligations. Educational programs and compliance training can help these entities remain aware of their responsibilities and the procedures for adherence.

COMPLIANCE AUDITS AND REVIEWS

Regular audits and reviews are essential to ensure that all parties comply with the set regulations. These audits should be conducted by independent bodies to ensure impartiality.

1. Regular Auditing: Regular audits of digital transactions and the technologies supporting CBDCs should be mandated to ensure that compliance systems are functioning as intended.

2. Feedback Mechanisms: Establishing robust feedback mechanisms can help regulatory bodies understand the challenges entities face in complying with regulations and adjust the regulatory frameworks accordingly.

Ensuring compliance in the digital financial world requires a multifaceted approach that combines revised regulatory frameworks, advanced technology utilization, international cooperation, focused training, and rigorous auditing. As the adoption of CBDCs progresses, continuous evaluation and adaptation of compliance strategies will be necessary to address emerging challenges and ensure that the digital financial ecosystem remains secure, transparent, and equitable.

The evolution of digital financial technologies, especially CBDCs, presents an ongoing challenge for regulatory frameworks, which must be dynamic and responsive to the rapid pace of technological change. Ensuring compliance in this environment not only involves adapting existing laws but also anticipating future developments and creating systems that can quickly adapt to new challenges.

PROACTIVE REGULATORY APPROACHES

To stay ahead of the curve, regulators must adopt proactive approaches, anticipating potential risks and issues before they materialize. This involves:

1. Scenario Planning and Stress Testing: Regular scenario planning and stress testing can help regulators understand potential future situations that could challenge CBDC systems. These exercises should be comprehensive, considering various risk factors including technological failures, market manipulations, and changes in user behavior due to macroeconomic factors.

2. Consultative Lawmaking: Engaging with a broad range of stakeholders, including tech developers, financial institutions, consumer groups, and academic experts, can provide regulators with diverse perspectives and expertise. This consultative approach ensures that new regulations are well-rounded and consider the interests and concerns of all affected parties.

3. Adaptive Legal Frameworks: Designing laws and regulations that are flexible and adaptable allows for quick adjustments in response to new information or technological innovations. This might involve the creation of modular legal frameworks that can be updated without overhauling the entire regulatory system.

INTEGRATING ADVANCED TECHNOLOGIES IN COMPLIANCE

The same technologies driving the development of CBDCs can also enhance regulatory and compliance processes. By integrating advanced technologies, regulators can improve the efficiency and effectiveness of compliance monitoring and enforcement.

1. Distributed Ledger for Transparency: Using distributed ledger technology not only for CBDC transactions but also for regulatory reporting could provide regulators with real-time access to data, enhancing the transparency and timeliness of compliance monitoring.

2. AI and Analytics for Pattern Detection: Artificial intelligence (AI) can be employed to analyze transaction patterns across the CBDC network to detect anomalies that may indicate fraudulent activity or deviations from expected patterns. These tools can automate the detection of potential compliance issues, allowing human regulators to focus on investigation and enforcement.

3. Automation of Compliance Processes: Automating routine compliance checks can reduce the workload on human regulators and decrease the time lag in identifying and addressing compliance issues. Automated systems can continuously monitor transactions and flag issues based on pre-defined criteria.

STRENGTHENING GLOBAL PARTNERSHIPS AND HARMONIZATION

Given the global nature of financial transactions, international cooperation becomes crucial in the regulation of CBDCs. Strengthening partnerships and harmonizing regulations across borders can mitigate risks associated with discrepancies in national regulations.

1. International Regulatory Bodies: Enhancing the roles of international regulatory bodies can help develop and enforce global standards for CBDC transactions. These bodies can

facilitate the exchange of information and best practices among nations.

2. Bilateral and Multilateral Agreements: Forming agreements on the treatment of CBDC transactions can reduce the risk of regulatory arbitrage where entities exploit differences between national regulations. These agreements can also facilitate smoother international transactions and enhance cooperation in enforcement actions.

ONGOING PUBLIC ENGAGEMENT AND EDUCATION

Maintaining public trust in CBDCs is essential for their widespread acceptance and use. Continuous public engagement and education initiatives are crucial to ensure that users are informed about their rights, the protections in place, and how to use CBDCs securely and effectively.

1. Transparency Initiatives: Regularly publishing detailed reports on CBDC operations, audits, and compliance status can help maintain public trust and confidence in the digital currency system.

2. Public Education Campaigns: Conducting ongoing education campaigns to inform the public about the features, benefits, and risks of CBDCs, as well as their rights and responsibilities as users, can enhance the effective and safe use of digital currencies.

Ensuring compliance in a digital financial world characterized by CBDCs involves a complex interplay of updated regulations, advanced technological integration, international cooperation, and robust public engagement. By adopting a proactive, inclusive, and technologically advanced regulatory approach, policymakers and regulators can create a stable, secure, and efficient environment for the operation of CBDCs. Such an environment not only supports the smooth function of the digital economy but also safeguards the interests of all stakeholders involved.

CHAPTER 8: GLOBAL PERSPECTIVES AND COORDINATION

8.1 International Regulatory Landscapes for CBDCs

As Central Bank Digital Currencies (CBDCs) continue to gain traction globally, understanding the international regulatory landscapes becomes imperative. This complex mosaic of regulatory frameworks reflects diverse economic, political, and technological environments across countries. Effective coordination and harmonization of these regulatory landscapes are crucial for the seamless global operation of CBDCs, fostering international trade, financial inclusion, and economic stability. This section explores the varying approaches to CBDC regulation worldwide and discusses the importance of international cooperation.

DIVERSE APPROACHES TO CBDC REGULATION

Different countries have embarked on CBDC projects with varied regulatory philosophies and goals, influenced by their unique financial systems, levels of technological advancement, and monetary policies.

1. United States: The discussion around CBDCs in the U.S. has been cautious and exploratory. Regulatory concerns focus

on ensuring privacy, security, and preventing illicit financial activities. The Federal Reserve has prioritized studying the potential impacts of a digital dollar on financial stability and the existing monetary system without committing to a specific rollout plan.

2. European Union: The European Central Bank (ECB) is advancing its digital euro project with a strong emphasis on privacy, transparency, and accessibility. The regulatory approach aims to complement existing financial systems without replacing cash. The ECB is actively engaging with stakeholders to establish a regulatory framework that supports innovation while addressing risks like money laundering and cyber threats.

3. China: As a front-runner in CBDC implementation, China's digital yuan is positioned to enhance state control over the monetary system and improve financial inclusion. The regulatory framework is tightly controlled by the People's Bank of China, focusing on widespread adoption within national borders and exploring cross-border usage. Privacy concerns and state surveillance are paramount in the regulatory discussions.

4. Bahamas: The Bahamas 'Sand Dollar, one of the first fully deployed CBDCs, aims to increase financial accessibility across its many islands. The regulatory framework emphasizes financial inclusion, operational resilience, and interoperability with existing financial institutions.

5. Japan: Japan has shown a strong interest in CBDCs, with the Bank of Japan (BoJ) conducting extensive research and pilot projects. The BoJ's regulatory approach focuses on ensuring that a digital yen can coexist with the current financial system and enhance payment efficiency. Japan's robust technological infrastructure provides a solid foundation for the implementation of CBDCs, yet regulatory efforts are aimed at addressing cybersecurity and financial stability concerns.

6. United Kingdom: The Bank of England (BoE) is actively exploring the potential of a digital pound. The BoE's regulatory considerations include safeguarding financial stability, ensuring robust cybersecurity measures, and maintaining monetary sovereignty. The UK's regulatory framework is likely to emphasize strong consumer protections and seamless integration with the existing financial ecosystem.

7. Sweden: Sweden's Riksbank is one of the pioneers in CBDC exploration with its e-Krona project. The Riksbank aims to ensure that the digital currency complements the declining use of cash while maintaining financial stability. The regulatory focus includes addressing the digital divide and ensuring that the e-Krona is accessible to all citizens, including the elderly and those in remote areas.

Cross-Border Initiatives: Various international collaborations are underway to test and develop cross-border CBDC solutions. For instance, the BIS Innovation Hub, along with central banks from different countries, is engaged in multiple projects to explore the interoperability of CBDCs across borders. These initiatives are crucial for establishing standardized protocols and ensuring smooth international transactions.

CHALLENGES IN INTERNATIONAL REGULATORY LANDSCAPES

The international regulatory environments for CBDCs present several challenges:

- Divergence in Regulatory Standards: Different countries have varying priorities and risks, leading to divergent regulatory standards. This divergence can complicate international transactions and pose challenges for multinational corporations and banks operating in multiple jurisdictions.

- Cross-border Payments and Settlements: The lack of standardized regulations can hinder the efficiency of cross-border payments and settlements. Discrepancies in CBDC regulations may lead to increased transaction costs and slower processing times, affecting global trade and economic cooperation.

- Data Privacy and Security: With differing legal standards on data protection across countries, international cooperation becomes complex. Ensuring the security and privacy of cross-border digital currency transactions while complying with multinational legal frameworks is a significant challenge.

To address these challenges, there is a critical need for international coordination and cooperation:

1. Establishing Common Standards: International bodies like the International Monetary Fund (IMF), the World Bank, and the Bank for International Settlements (BIS) can play a pivotal role in developing common standards for CBDCs. These standards could address technical specifications, security protocols, and legal compliance requirements, facilitating smoother international transactions.

2. Harmonizing Regulatory Frameworks: Through global forums and multinational agreements, countries can work towards harmonizing their regulatory frameworks. This harmonization can help mitigate the risks of regulatory arbitrage, where entities exploit differences between national regulations to circumvent controls.

3. Joint Development and Testing Initiatives: Countries can collaborate on joint development and testing initiatives to share knowledge, technologies, and best practices. These collaborative efforts can accelerate CBDC development, reduce costs, and ensure that emerging best practices are widely adopted.

Understanding and navigating the international regulatory landscapes for CBDCs is crucial for their successful global integration. While the diversity in regulatory approaches reflects the unique needs and conditions of different countries, international coordination and cooperation are essential to address the challenges of cross-border transactions, regulatory divergence, and data privacy. By fostering a collaborative international environment, countries can leverage the benefits of CBDCs to enhance global financial stability, promote economic development, and facilitate international trade.

ACTIONABLE STEPS FOR ENHANCED INTERNATIONAL COOPERATION

1. Creating a Global Regulatory Framework: A global regulatory framework for CBDCs, developed under the auspices of international financial institutions such as the IMF, BIS, and the World Bank, can provide a cohesive set of guidelines that countries can adapt to their specific contexts. This framework should address key issues such as data privacy, AML/CTF measures, cybersecurity, and consumer protection.

2. Establishing CBDC Working Groups: Forming international CBDC working groups that include representatives from central banks, financial regulators, and technology experts can facilitate knowledge sharing and collaborative problem-solving. These working groups can focus on specific challenges such as cross-border interoperability, regulatory harmonization, and technological advancements.

3. Conducting Joint Pilots and Research: Countries can engage in joint pilot programs and research initiatives to test cross-border CBDC functionalities. These collaborative projects can provide valuable insights into operational challenges, user adoption, and regulatory compliance. The findings can inform the development of international standards and best practices.

4. Standardizing Technological Protocols: Developing standardized technological protocols for CBDCs can ensure compatibility and interoperability across different systems. These standards should cover aspects such as digital wallet infrastructure, encryption methods, and transaction

processing. International organizations can spearhead the development of these standards.

5. Promoting Regulatory Sandboxes: Encouraging the use of regulatory sandboxes for CBDCs can help central banks and regulators test new technologies and regulatory approaches in a controlled environment. International coordination of these sandboxes can facilitate the exchange of experiences and accelerate the development of effective regulatory practices.

6. Enhancing Cybersecurity Collaboration: Given the critical importance of cybersecurity in the digital financial landscape, countries should collaborate on developing robust cybersecurity frameworks for CBDCs. This includes sharing threat intelligence, conducting joint cybersecurity exercises, and establishing international protocols for responding to cyber incidents.

7. Building Public Awareness and Trust: International efforts should also focus on building public awareness and trust in CBDCs. Coordinated public education campaigns can help demystify digital currencies, explain their benefits and risks, and promote responsible usage. Ensuring transparency in regulatory processes and maintaining high standards of consumer protection are key to gaining public confidence.

8. Monitoring and Evaluation: Establishing mechanisms for ongoing monitoring and evaluation of CBDC implementations can help identify emerging risks and best practices. International bodies can play a role in coordinating these efforts, ensuring that lessons learned are shared globally and that regulatory frameworks remain adaptive to new challenges.

The successful global integration of CBDCs hinges on effective international coordination and cooperation. While countries may have unique regulatory approaches based on their specific needs and circumstances, harmonizing these efforts through a global regulatory framework, collaborative research, and standardized technological protocols can facilitate the seamless operation of CBDCs worldwide. By addressing challenges such as cross-border payments, data privacy, and cybersecurity, and by promoting public trust and awareness, the international community can harness the potential of CBDCs to enhance financial inclusion, stability, and efficiency in the global financial system.

8.2 Case Studies: Different Approaches to CBDC Regulation

To understand the diverse regulatory landscapes for Central Bank Digital Currencies (CBDCs), it is essential to examine case studies from various countries that have embarked on their digital currency journeys. These case studies illustrate different approaches to CBDC regulation, highlighting the challenges faced, the solutions implemented, and the lessons learned. By exploring these examples, we can gain valuable insights into the complexity and nuances of regulating digital currencies.

CASE STUDY 1: CHINA'S DIGITAL YUAN

China has been a frontrunner in the development and implementation of a CBDC, known as the digital yuan or e-CNY. The People's Bank of China (PBoC) has taken a proactive approach, focusing on widespread adoption and integration into the existing financial system.

Regulatory Approach:

- State Control: The PBoC maintains strict control over the issuance and distribution of the digital yuan. This centralized approach ensures that the state can monitor and regulate all transactions, helping to prevent illicit activities and maintain financial stability.
- Privacy and Surveillance: While the digital yuan aims to protect user privacy to some extent, it also incorporates features that allow for extensive state surveillance. This dual approach

helps balance user privacy with the need for regulatory oversight.
- Pilot Programs: China has conducted extensive pilot programs in various cities, testing the digital yuan in different scenarios and refining the technology and regulatory frameworks based on real-world feedback.

Challenges and Solutions:

- Public Trust: Ensuring public trust in the digital yuan required extensive public education campaigns and transparency about the currency's features and benefits.
- Technological Integration: Integrating the digital yuan with existing financial systems and payment platforms involved significant technological investments and collaboration with private sector partners.

CASE STUDY 2: SWEDEN'S E-KRONA

Sweden's Riksbank has been exploring the concept of the e-Krona to address the declining use of cash and ensure the public has access to state-backed digital money.

Regulatory Approach:

- Complementary Role: The e-Krona is designed to complement cash and other forms of digital payment rather than replace them, ensuring that all citizens can access central bank money.
- Consumer Protection: Strong emphasis is placed on consumer protection, ensuring that users have clear rights and recourse in the event of fraud or errors.
- Technological Inclusivity: Efforts are made to ensure that the e-Krona is accessible to all segments of the population, including those who may not be technologically savvy.

Challenges and Solutions:

- Digital Divide: Addressing the digital divide involved creating user-friendly interfaces and providing support and education to

ensure that all citizens can use the e-Krona effectively.
- Financial Stability: Ensuring that the introduction of the e-Krona does not disrupt the existing financial system required careful planning and phased implementation.

CASE STUDY 3: THE BAHAMAS 'SAND DOLLAR

The Bahamas launched the Sand Dollar to enhance financial inclusion and improve the resilience of its financial system, especially given the geographical challenges posed by its many islands.

Regulatory Approach:

- Financial Inclusion: The regulatory framework focuses on ensuring that all citizens, including those in remote areas, can access the Sand Dollar. This includes partnering with mobile network operators to facilitate digital transactions.
- Resilience and Security: Emphasis is placed on ensuring the security and resilience of the Sand Dollar system, protecting against cyber threats and ensuring operational continuity.
- Interoperability: The Sand Dollar is designed to be interoperable with existing banking systems and digital payment platforms, facilitating widespread adoption.

Challenges and Solutions:

- Geographical Barriers: Overcoming geographical barriers involved leveraging mobile technology and ensuring offline transaction capabilities.
- Public Awareness: Building public awareness and trust in the Sand Dollar required extensive outreach and education efforts.

CASE STUDY 4: EUROPEAN CENTRAL BANK'S DIGITAL EURO

The European Central Bank (ECB) is exploring the digital euro with the aim of ensuring that European citizens have access to a secure and efficient form of digital central bank money.

Regulatory Approach:

- Privacy and Security: The ECB places a strong emphasis on protecting user privacy while ensuring that the digital euro is secure and resilient against cyber threats.
- Monetary Sovereignty: Ensuring that the digital euro complements existing monetary policies and maintains the ECB's control over the monetary system is a key regulatory focus.
- Stakeholder Engagement: The ECB engages extensively with stakeholders, including financial institutions, technology providers, and the public, to ensure that the digital euro meets diverse needs and expectations.

Challenges and Solutions:

- Balancing Privacy and Regulation: Balancing the need for user privacy with regulatory requirements for transparency and anti-money laundering measures required innovative solutions, such as tiered privacy levels for different types of transactions.
- Technical and Legal Harmonization: Ensuring that the digital euro can be used seamlessly across all Eurozone countries involved harmonizing technical standards and legal frameworks.

CASE STUDY 5: CANADA'S PROJECT JASPER

Canada's Project Jasper explores the use of blockchain technology for wholesale payments, with a focus on improving the efficiency and security of interbank settlements.

Regulatory Approach:

- Collaborative Development: The Bank of Canada collaborates with commercial banks and technology providers to develop and test the CBDC system, ensuring that it meets the needs of all stakeholders.
- Focus on Efficiency: The regulatory framework aims to enhance the efficiency of the financial system, reducing settlement times and operational costs.

- Robust Security Measures: Strong security measures are integrated into the system to protect against cyber threats and ensure the integrity of financial transactions.

Challenges and Solutions:

- Interbank Coordination: Coordinating with multiple banks and financial institutions to ensure seamless integration and operation involved extensive collaboration and testing.
- Scalability: Ensuring that the system can handle large volumes of transactions without compromising security or efficiency required significant technological investments.

These case studies illustrate the diverse approaches to CBDC regulation across different countries. Each regulatory framework reflects the unique economic, technological, and social conditions of the respective countries. Despite these differences, common themes such as the importance of financial inclusion, the need for robust security measures, and the value of stakeholder engagement emerge across all case studies. By learning from these varied experiences, other nations can develop effective regulatory frameworks that address their specific needs while contributing to the global discourse on CBDCs.

8.3 Strategies for Global Regulatory Harmonization

The successful implementation and operation of Central Bank Digital Currencies (CBDCs) on a global scale depend heavily on harmonized regulatory frameworks. Without consistent international standards, the benefits of CBDCs could be undermined by fragmentation, inefficiencies, and potential regulatory arbitrage. This section outlines strategies for achieving global regulatory harmonization for CBDCs, which will facilitate seamless cross-border transactions, enhance financial stability, and foster international cooperation.

1. Establishing International Standards and Protocols

To ensure interoperability and uniformity, international financial bodies such as the International Monetary Fund (IMF), Bank for International Settlements (BIS), and the Financial Stability Board (FSB) should take the lead in developing comprehensive standards for CBDCs. These standards should cover:

- Technical Specifications: Defining protocols for transaction processing, data security, interoperability, and system resilience.
- Regulatory Requirements: Establishing common guidelines for anti-money laundering (AML), counter-terrorism financing (CTF), consumer protection, and data privacy.
- Operational Procedures: Standardizing the processes for issuing, distributing, and redeeming CBDCs, as well as for handling cross-border transactions.

2. Creating a Global Regulatory Framework

A global regulatory framework for CBDCs should be designed to provide a cohesive set of principles that individual countries can adapt to their specific contexts. This framework should be developed through collaborative efforts involving central banks, regulatory authorities, and international organizations. Key elements of this framework include:

- Legal Clarity: Defining the legal status of CBDCs, their acceptance as legal tender, and their role in the monetary system.
- Compliance Mechanisms: Establishing uniform compliance requirements for financial institutions and other stakeholders involved in the issuance and management of CBDCs.
- Dispute Resolution: Developing international mechanisms for resolving disputes related to CBDC transactions and regulatory compliance.

3. Facilitating Cross-Border Collaboration

Countries should engage in cross-border collaboration to address the challenges of CBDC implementation and regulation. This collaboration can take various forms, including:

- Bilateral and Multilateral Agreements: Negotiating agreements that facilitate the mutual recognition of regulatory standards and the smooth execution of cross-border transactions.
- Joint Research and Development: Conducting collaborative research projects and pilot programs to test and refine CBDC technologies and regulatory approaches.
- Regulatory Sandboxes: Establishing cross-border regulatory sandboxes that allow for the controlled testing of new CBDC applications and compliance mechanisms.

4. Enhancing Information Sharing and Coordination

Effective harmonization requires robust mechanisms for information sharing and coordination among regulatory bodies. Strategies to achieve this include:

- Regular Consultations: Holding regular meetings and consultations among central banks and regulatory authorities to discuss progress, challenges, and best practices in CBDC implementation.
- Data Sharing Platforms: Developing secure platforms for the exchange of information on regulatory compliance, transaction monitoring, and cybersecurity threats.
- Joint Training Programs: Organizing joint training programs and workshops for regulators and financial institutions to enhance their understanding of CBDC technologies and regulatory requirements.

5. Addressing Cybersecurity and Privacy Concerns

Given the digital nature of CBDCs, cybersecurity and data privacy are critical concerns that require harmonized approaches. Strategies to address these concerns include:

- Global Cybersecurity Standards: Developing and enforcing international cybersecurity standards that protect CBDC systems from cyber threats and ensure the integrity of transactions.
- Privacy Frameworks: Establishing international privacy frameworks that balance the need for transaction transparency with the protection of individual privacy rights.
- Incident Response Protocols: Creating coordinated protocols for responding to cybersecurity incidents and data breaches, including mechanisms for cross-border cooperation and information sharing.

6. Promoting Public Awareness and Trust

Building public trust in CBDCs is essential for their widespread adoption and effective operation. Harmonized efforts to promote public awareness and trust should include:

- Public Education Campaigns: Conducting international campaigns to educate the public about the benefits, risks, and proper use of CBDCs.
- Transparency Initiatives: Ensuring transparency in the development and implementation of CBDC policies and technologies, including regular updates and public consultations.
- Consumer Protection Measures: Implementing robust consumer protection measures that safeguard users 'interests and build confidence in the safety and reliability of CBDCs.

7. Monitoring and Evaluation

Continuous monitoring and evaluation are crucial for ensuring that regulatory frameworks remain effective and responsive to new challenges. Strategies for ongoing monitoring and evaluation include:

- International Monitoring Bodies: Establishing international

bodies to monitor the implementation and impact of CBDC regulations, providing regular reports and recommendations for improvement.
- Feedback Mechanisms: Creating mechanisms for collecting feedback from stakeholders, including financial institutions, technology providers, and consumers, to inform regulatory adjustments.
- Adaptive Regulations: Designing regulations that are flexible and adaptable, allowing for timely updates in response to technological advancements and evolving market conditions.

Achieving global regulatory harmonization for CBDCs is a complex but essential task that requires coordinated efforts across multiple dimensions. By establishing international standards, creating a cohesive regulatory framework, facilitating cross-border collaboration, enhancing information sharing, addressing cybersecurity and privacy concerns, promoting public awareness, and ensuring continuous monitoring and evaluation, the international community can support the successful implementation and operation of CBDCs. These efforts will not only facilitate seamless cross-border transactions and enhance financial stability but also foster innovation and inclusivity in the global financial system.

8.4 The Role of Supranational Organizations

Supranational organizations play a critical role in the development, regulation, and harmonization of Central Bank Digital Currencies (CBDCs). These entities, which operate above the national level and include bodies such as the International Monetary Fund (IMF), the Bank for International Settlements (BIS), the Financial Stability Board (FSB), and the World Bank, provide the necessary frameworks, guidance, and coordination for ensuring that CBDCs are implemented effectively and harmoniously across different jurisdictions. This section explores the pivotal roles these organizations play in shaping the global landscape for CBDCs.

1. Developing International Standards and Guidelines

One of the primary roles of supranational organizations is to develop international standards and guidelines for CBDCs. These standards ensure that CBDCs are interoperable, secure, and compliant with global financial norms.

- IMF and BIS: Both the IMF and BIS have been at the forefront of research and policy development for CBDCs. They provide crucial insights into the design, implementation, and potential impacts of CBDCs on global financial stability and economic policy.
- FSB: The FSB works on setting global standards for financial regulation, including the regulation of digital currencies. By developing comprehensive guidelines for CBDCs, the FSB ensures that these digital currencies do not pose undue risks to financial stability.

2. Facilitating Cross-Border Cooperation

Supranational organizations are instrumental in fostering cross-border cooperation, which is essential for the seamless operation of CBDCs in a globally interconnected financial system.

- Coordination of Regulatory Efforts: These organizations facilitate the harmonization of regulatory frameworks across different countries, ensuring that there are no significant regulatory arbitrage opportunities that could be exploited.
- Joint Research and Development: They support joint research initiatives and pilot projects involving multiple countries, helping to test and refine CBDC technologies and regulatory approaches in a collaborative manner.

3. Providing Technical Assistance and Capacity Building

Supranational organizations offer technical assistance and capacity-building support to countries that are developing and implementing CBDCs. This is particularly important for emerging and developing economies that may lack the necessary expertise and resources.

- World Bank: The World Bank provides technical assistance to countries in areas such as digital infrastructure development, cybersecurity, and financial inclusion. By helping these countries build the necessary foundations, the World Bank ensures that CBDCs can be deployed effectively and inclusively.
- Capacity Building Programs: Organizations like the IMF and BIS conduct training programs, workshops, and seminars to enhance the capacity of central banks and financial regulators to manage CBDCs. These programs cover a range of topics, including regulatory compliance, technological innovation, and risk management.

4. Ensuring Financial Stability and Security

The stability and security of the global financial system are paramount concerns for supranational organizations. They play a key role in ensuring that CBDCs do not compromise these objectives.

- Risk Assessment and Mitigation: The IMF and BIS conduct extensive risk assessments to identify potential threats posed by CBDCs to financial stability. They develop frameworks and tools to help countries mitigate these risks effectively.
- Cybersecurity Standards: Supranational organizations also set high standards for cybersecurity, ensuring that CBDC systems are resilient against cyber threats. They promote the adoption of best practices and technologies to safeguard digital currencies.

5. Promoting Financial Inclusion and Development

CBDCs have the potential to enhance financial inclusion, particularly in regions where access to traditional banking services is limited. Supranational organizations advocate for the use of CBDCs as tools for promoting inclusive growth and development.

- Inclusive Design Principles: The World Bank and IMF promote the adoption of CBDCs that are designed with inclusivity in mind, ensuring that these digital currencies are accessible to all segments of the population, including the unbanked and underbanked.
- Development Projects: These organizations support development projects that leverage CBDCs to improve access to financial services, reduce transaction costs, and stimulate economic activity in underserved regions.

6. Enhancing Transparency and Accountability

Transparency and accountability are crucial for building public trust in CBDCs. Supranational organizations work to ensure that CBDC implementations are transparent and that there is accountability in their management.

- Transparent Reporting: Organizations like the IMF and BIS advocate for transparent reporting on CBDC projects, including public disclosures of objectives, progress, and outcomes. This transparency helps build confidence in the integrity and reliability of CBDCs.
- Accountability Mechanisms: They also promote the establishment of accountability mechanisms, such as independent audits and oversight bodies, to ensure that CBDCs are managed in a responsible and ethical manner.

7. Encouraging Innovation and Adaptability

Supranational organizations encourage innovation in the development and deployment of CBDCs, ensuring that these digital currencies remain adaptable to evolving technological and economic conditions.

- Innovation Hubs: The BIS, through its Innovation Hub,

supports innovative projects that explore new applications of digital currencies and related technologies. These initiatives help push the boundaries of what is possible with CBDCs and ensure that they continue to evolve in response to new challenges and opportunities.

- Adaptive Regulations: These organizations advocate for regulatory frameworks that are flexible and adaptable, allowing for the incorporation of new technologies and practices as they emerge.

Supranational organizations play an indispensable role in the global development and regulation of CBDCs. By setting international standards, facilitating cross-border cooperation, providing technical assistance, ensuring financial stability, promoting financial inclusion, enhancing transparency, and encouraging innovation, these organizations help create a coherent and effective framework for CBDCs. Their efforts ensure that digital currencies can fulfill their potential as secure, inclusive, and efficient means of payment in the global financial system. Through continued collaboration and leadership, supranational organizations will remain pivotal in navigating the complexities and opportunities presented by the rise of CBDCs.

CHAPTER 9: TECHNOLOGICAL SOLUTIONS FOR CBDCS

9.1 Blockchain and Distributed Ledger Technology

The implementation of Central Bank Digital Currencies (CBDCs) hinges significantly on robust technological foundations. Among the various technological solutions available, Blockchain and Distributed Ledger Technology (DLT) stand out due to their potential to offer transparency, security, and efficiency. Understanding the role of blockchain and DLT in CBDC systems requires an exploration of their fundamental principles, their benefits, challenges, and real-world applications in the context of digital currencies.

Blockchain technology is a type of distributed ledger where transactions are recorded in blocks and linked chronologically to form a continuous chain. This structure ensures that all participants in the network share a synchronized ledger that is immutable and transparent. The decentralized nature of blockchain means that no single entity controls the entire ledger, thereby reducing the risk of fraud and manipulation. Each block in the blockchain contains a cryptographic hash of the previous block, a timestamp, and transaction data, making it highly resistant to tampering.

Distributed Ledger Technology, while closely related to blockchain, encompasses a broader range of technologies that enable the recording, sharing, and synchronization of transactions across a distributed network of participants. Unlike traditional databases, which are centrally controlled, DLT allows for multiple copies of the ledger to be maintained by different participants. This decentralized approach enhances security and resilience, as there is no single point of failure.

The application of blockchain and DLT in CBDCs offers several significant benefits. One of the primary advantages is enhanced security. The cryptographic nature of blockchain ensures that transactions are secure and tamper-proof. Each transaction is validated by network participants through consensus mechanisms, such as proof of work or proof of stake, which makes unauthorized changes to the ledger nearly impossible. This high level of security is crucial for maintaining trust in the digital currency.

Transparency is another key benefit of blockchain and DLT. All transactions recorded on the blockchain are visible to all participants, ensuring full transparency. This visibility can help prevent fraud and other illicit activities by making it easier to track and audit transactions. Moreover, the immutable nature of blockchain means that once a transaction is recorded, it cannot be altered or deleted, providing a reliable and verifiable history of all transactions.

Efficiency is also a notable advantage of using blockchain and DLT for CBDCs. Traditional financial systems often involve multiple intermediaries, which can slow down transaction processing and increase costs. In contrast, blockchain-based systems can facilitate direct peer-to-peer transactions, reducing the need for intermediaries and enabling faster and cheaper transactions. Smart contracts, which are self-executing contracts with the terms of the agreement directly written into code, can further enhance efficiency by automating processes and reducing the potential for human error.

Despite these benefits, the implementation of blockchain and DLT in CBDCs also presents several challenges. One of the main concerns is scalability. Blockchain networks, particularly those that use proof of work consensus mechanisms, can face limitations in processing large volumes of transactions quickly. This issue, often referred to as the scalability trilemma, involves balancing scalability, security, and decentralization. Finding a solution that allows for high transaction throughput without compromising security and decentralization is a critical challenge for CBDC systems.

Energy consumption is another significant challenge associated with blockchain technology. Proof of work consensus mechanisms, used by cryptocurrencies like Bitcoin, require substantial computational power, leading to high energy consumption. This environmental impact is a growing concern, especially as the global community seeks to reduce carbon emissions and promote sustainable practices. Exploring alternative consensus mechanisms, such as proof of stake or other energy-efficient protocols, is essential for making blockchain-based CBDCs more sustainable.

Interoperability is also a critical consideration. For CBDCs to be effective, they need to be interoperable with existing financial systems and other digital currencies. Ensuring seamless integration and interoperability requires the development of common standards and protocols. Without interoperability, the adoption of CBDCs could be hindered by fragmentation and inefficiencies in the financial system.

Real-world applications of blockchain and DLT in CBDCs are already underway, providing valuable insights and lessons.

For example, China's digital yuan, known as e-CNY, leverages blockchain technology to ensure secure and transparent transactions. The People's Bank of China has conducted extensive pilot programs to test the digital yuan in various scenarios, including retail payments, salary distribution, and cross-border transactions. These pilots have demonstrated the potential of blockchain to enhance the efficiency and security of the financial system.

Sweden's e-Krona project is another example of blockchain application in CBDCs. The Riksbank has explored the use of blockchain to support the e-Krona, aiming to provide a digital complement to cash. The e-Krona pilot has focused on ensuring that the digital currency is accessible to all citizens, including those without access to traditional banking services. By leveraging blockchain technology, the Riksbank aims to create a secure and inclusive digital payment system.

In the Caribbean, the Eastern Caribbean Central Bank (ECCB) launched DCash, a blockchain-based digital currency aimed at enhancing financial inclusion and reducing transaction costs. DCash is designed to be used across multiple island nations within the Eastern Caribbean Currency Union, providing a seamless and efficient payment solution. The ECCB's use of blockchain technology ensures that transactions are secure and transparent, fostering trust and confidence in the digital currency.

The Bahamas' Sand Dollar also utilizes blockchain technology to enhance financial inclusion and resilience. By leveraging a secure and transparent blockchain infrastructure, the Central Bank of The Bahamas has ensured that the Sand Dollar can be used effectively across the archipelago, including in remote and underserved areas. The Sand Dollar's success demonstrates the potential of blockchain to address unique geographical and economic challenges.

These real-world applications highlight the versatility and potential of blockchain and DLT in CBDC systems. However, they also underscore the importance of addressing the associated challenges to fully realize the benefits of digital currencies. Continued research and development, as well as collaboration among central banks, technology providers, and regulatory bodies, are essential for overcoming these challenges.

Blockchain and Distributed Ledger Technology offer significant advantages for the implementation of Central Bank Digital Currencies, including enhanced security, transparency, and efficiency. However, the successful deployment of blockchain-based CBDCs requires addressing challenges related to scalability, energy consumption, and interoperability. Real-world applications provide valuable insights and demonstrate the potential of these technologies to transform the financial system. By continuing to explore and refine blockchain and DLT, central banks can harness their potential to create secure, efficient, and inclusive digital currencies that meet the evolving needs of the global economy.

9.2 Smart Contracts and Their Applications

Smart contracts represent a transformative technology that can significantly enhance the functionality, security, and efficiency of Central Bank Digital Currencies (CBDCs). A smart contract is a self-executing contract with the terms of the agreement directly written into code. These contracts are stored on a blockchain, ensuring that they are immutable and transparent. By automatically enforcing the terms of an agreement, smart contracts eliminate the need for intermediaries, reduce the risk of human error, and facilitate more efficient and secure transactions.

The concept of smart contracts was first proposed by computer scientist Nick Szabo in the 1990s. Szabo envisioned these contracts as a way to digitally facilitate, verify, or enforce the negotiation or performance of a contract. With the advent of blockchain technology, Szabo's vision has become a reality, enabling the development of complex financial instruments and automated processes that operate with minimal human intervention.

In the context of CBDCs, smart contracts can be used to streamline a wide range of financial transactions and processes. One of the most significant applications is in the automation of payments. For instance, a smart contract could be used to automatically transfer CBDCs from a payer to a payee upon the completion of a predefined condition, such as the delivery of goods or services. This automated process reduces the need for manual verification and processing, speeding up transactions and reducing administrative costs.

Another important application of smart contracts in CBDCs is in the realm of programmable money. Programmable money allows for the customization of currency to perform specific functions based on predefined criteria. For example, CBDCs could be programmed to be spent only on certain goods or services, or to expire after a certain period if not used. This feature is particularly useful for distributing government benefits, subsidies, or stimulus payments, ensuring that funds are used for their intended purposes and within a specified timeframe.

Smart contracts can also play a crucial role in enhancing financial inclusion. By automating complex financial processes, smart contracts can reduce barriers to entry for individuals and businesses that may lack access to traditional financial services. For example, microloans and other financial products can be issued and managed through smart contracts, providing underserved populations with access to credit and other essential financial services. This automation reduces the costs and complexities associated with traditional banking, making financial services more accessible and affordable.

In addition to enhancing efficiency and inclusivity, smart contracts can improve the transparency and accountability of financial transactions. Since smart contracts are executed on a blockchain, all transactions are recorded in an immutable ledger that is accessible to all participants. This transparency ensures that all parties can verify the terms and execution of the contract, reducing the risk of fraud and disputes. Furthermore, the immutable nature of blockchain records provides a reliable audit trail, facilitating regulatory compliance and oversight.

The use of smart contracts in CBDCs also has significant implications for cross-border transactions. Traditional cross-border payments can be slow, costly, and subject to regulatory complexities. Smart contracts can streamline these processes by automating the execution of cross-border payments based on predefined conditions. For example, a smart contract could automatically convert one CBDC to another at a predefined exchange rate and transfer the funds to the recipient upon confirmation of receipt of goods. This automation reduces the need for intermediaries, lowers transaction costs, and speeds up the settlement process.

Despite their numerous benefits, the implementation of smart contracts in CBDCs is not without challenges. One of the primary concerns is the security and reliability of smart contract code. Since smart contracts are self-executing, any errors or vulnerabilities in the code can lead to unintended consequences or exploitation by malicious actors. Ensuring the security and reliability of smart contracts requires rigorous testing, auditing, and verification of the code. Additionally, mechanisms for updating or modifying smart contracts in response to changing circumstances or discovered vulnerabilities must be in place.

Another challenge is the legal and regulatory framework for smart contracts. Traditional legal systems are not always well-equipped to handle disputes or enforce agreements that are codified in smart contracts. Establishing a clear legal framework that recognizes the validity and enforceability of smart contracts is essential for their widespread adoption. This framework must address issues such as jurisdiction, liability, and the resolution of disputes arising from the execution of smart contracts.

Interoperability is also a critical consideration for the implementation of smart contracts in CBDCs. For smart contracts to be effective, they must be able to interact with different blockchain platforms and financial systems. Developing common standards and protocols for smart contracts can ensure that they are interoperable and can be seamlessly integrated into existing financial infrastructures. This interoperability is particularly important for cross-border transactions, where different countries may have different technological and regulatory environments.

Real-world applications of smart contracts in CBDCs are already beginning to emerge, providing valuable insights into their potential and challenges. For example, the Bank of France has conducted experiments using smart contracts to settle government bond transactions. These experiments demonstrated that smart contracts could automate the entire lifecycle of a bond transaction, from issuance to settlement, significantly reducing processing times and operational risks.

Similarly, the Monetary Authority of Singapore (MAS) has explored the use of smart contracts in Project Ubin, a multi-phase initiative to explore the use of blockchain and DLT for clearing and settlement of payments and securities. In one of the phases, MAS tested the use of smart contracts to enable automated settlement of cross-border transactions. The results showed that smart contracts could streamline the settlement process, reduce the risk of errors, and enhance transparency.

In the Caribbean, the Eastern Caribbean Central Bank (ECCB) has incorporated smart contracts into its DCash project. The ECCB uses smart contracts to automate compliance with regulatory requirements, such as anti-money laundering (AML) and know-your-customer (KYC) checks. This automation ensures that transactions comply with regulatory standards, reducing the burden on financial institutions and enhancing the overall security of the digital currency system.

The potential applications of smart contracts in CBDCs are vast and varied. They can transform the way financial transactions are conducted, making them more efficient, transparent, and secure. However, realizing this potential requires addressing the challenges associated with smart contract implementation, including security, legal recognition, and interoperability. By continuing to explore and refine the use of smart contracts in CBDCs, central banks can harness their transformative power to create a more efficient and inclusive financial system.

Smart contracts represent a powerful tool for enhancing the functionality and efficiency of Central Bank Digital Currencies. Their ability to automate complex financial transactions, ensure transparency and accountability, and improve financial inclusion makes them a valuable component of CBDC systems. However, the successful implementation of smart contracts requires addressing challenges related to security, legal recognition, and interoperability. By continuing to explore real-world applications and developing robust frameworks for their use, central banks can leverage smart contracts to create a more efficient, secure, and inclusive financial system that meets the needs of the digital economy.

9.3 Ensuring Security and Privacy

in Digital Transactions

The transition to Central Bank Digital Currencies (CBDCs) introduces both opportunities and challenges in the realm of security and privacy. Ensuring the integrity of digital transactions and protecting user data are paramount for the successful adoption and operation of CBDCs. This section explores the various technological and regulatory strategies that can be employed to safeguard security and privacy in digital transactions.

At the heart of ensuring security in digital transactions is the use of advanced cryptographic techniques. Cryptography provides the foundational layer of security for CBDCs, enabling secure communication and data protection. Public key infrastructure (PKI) is widely used to ensure the authenticity and integrity of transactions. In PKI, each user has a pair of cryptographic keys: a public key, which is shared openly, and a private key, which is kept secret. When a transaction is made, it is signed with the sender's private key and can be verified by others using the sender's public key. This mechanism ensures that the transaction is authentic and has not been tampered with.

In addition to PKI, digital signatures and hashing algorithms play crucial roles in maintaining the security of digital transactions. Digital signatures provide a way to verify the identity of the sender and ensure the integrity of the transaction data. Hashing algorithms transform transaction data into a fixed-size string of characters, which serves as a unique digital fingerprint. Any alteration to the original data will result in a completely different hash, making it easy to detect any unauthorized changes.

Another essential aspect of securing digital transactions is the implementation of robust cybersecurity measures. As CBDCs operate within a digital environment, they are susceptible to various cyber threats, including hacking, phishing, and denial-of-service attacks. To mitigate these risks, central banks and financial institutions must adopt a multi-layered cybersecurity approach. This approach includes the use of firewalls, intrusion detection systems, and anti-malware software to protect the digital infrastructure. Regular security audits and vulnerability assessments are also critical to identify and address potential weaknesses in the system.

The use of decentralized networks, such as blockchain and distributed ledger technology (DLT), can enhance the security of CBDCs by eliminating single points of failure. In a decentralized network, transaction data is distributed across multiple nodes, making it difficult for malicious actors to compromise the entire system. Each node in the network maintains a copy of the ledger, and transactions are validated through consensus mechanisms. This decentralized approach not only improves security but also enhances the resilience and reliability of the digital currency system.

Privacy in digital transactions is equally important, as it involves protecting the personal and financial information of users. Ensuring privacy requires balancing transparency with confidentiality. While it is essential to have transparent transaction records for audit and compliance purposes, it is also crucial to safeguard sensitive user information from unauthorized access and misuse.

One approach to enhancing privacy in digital transactions is the use of zero-knowledge proofs (ZKPs). ZKPs are cryptographic protocols that allow one party to prove to another that a statement is true without revealing any additional information. In the context of CBDCs, ZKPs can be used to verify transactions without disclosing the details of the transaction to third parties. This ensures that the transaction is valid while preserving the privacy of the parties involved.

Another privacy-enhancing technology is homomorphic encryption, which allows computations to be performed on encrypted data without decrypting it. This means that financial institutions can process transactions and perform analyses on encrypted data without accessing the underlying sensitive information. Homomorphic encryption can help maintain privacy while still enabling necessary data processing and compliance checks.

The implementation of privacy-preserving technologies must be complemented by strong data protection regulations. Regulations such as the General Data Protection Regulation (GDPR) in the European Union set strict standards for the collection, processing, and storage of personal data. These regulations require organizations to obtain explicit consent from individuals before collecting their data, to use the data only for specified purposes, and to implement measures to protect the data from breaches. Ensuring compliance with such regulations is essential for maintaining user trust in CBDCs.

Access control mechanisms are also vital for ensuring both security and privacy in digital transactions. Role-based access control (RBAC) and attribute-based access control (ABAC) are commonly used to restrict access to sensitive data based on the roles and attributes of users. These mechanisms ensure that only authorized individuals can access or modify transaction data, reducing the risk of insider threats and unauthorized access.

Another critical aspect of ensuring security and privacy is the use of secure hardware devices, such as hardware security modules (HSMs) and secure elements (SEs). These devices provide a secure environment for storing cryptographic keys and executing sensitive operations. HSMs are typically used in server environments to protect cryptographic keys and perform encryption and decryption operations. SEs, on the other hand, are used in end-user devices, such as smartphones and smart cards, to securely store private keys and perform cryptographic operations.

In addition to technological measures, fostering a culture of security and privacy awareness is essential for the effective protection of digital transactions. Central banks and financial institutions must invest in training and awareness programs to educate their employees and customers about best practices for security and privacy. This includes training on recognizing phishing attempts, creating strong passwords, and securely handling sensitive information.

Collaboration and information sharing among financial institutions, regulatory bodies, and technology providers are also crucial for enhancing security and privacy. By sharing information about emerging threats, vulnerabilities, and best practices, organizations can collectively strengthen their defenses against cyber threats. Establishing industry standards and frameworks for security and privacy can further support these collaborative efforts.

Lastly, continuous monitoring and improvement are essential for maintaining the security and privacy of digital transactions. As cyber threats evolve, so too must the defenses against them. Regularly updating security protocols, conducting penetration tests, and reviewing privacy practices are critical for identifying and addressing new vulnerabilities. By adopting a proactive and adaptive approach, central banks and financial institutions can ensure that their digital currency systems remain secure and trustworthy.

Advanced cryptographic techniques, robust cybersecurity measures, decentralized networks, and privacy-enhancing technologies form the technological backbone of secure and private CBDCs. These technological solutions must be complemented by strong regulatory frameworks, access control mechanisms, secure hardware devices, and a culture of security and privacy awareness. Continuous monitoring, collaboration, and information sharing are also vital for staying ahead of emerging threats and maintaining user trust in digital currency systems. By addressing these challenges holistically, central banks can create secure, efficient, and private digital currencies that meet the evolving needs of the digital economy.

9.4 Integrating CBDCs with Existing Financial Systems

The integration of Central Bank Digital Currencies (CBDCs) with existing financial systems is a critical component of their successful implementation. This process requires careful planning and coordination to ensure that CBDCs complement and enhance current financial infrastructures rather than disrupt them. The seamless integration of CBDCs can lead to more efficient payment systems, enhanced financial inclusion, and improved monetary policy transmission. However, achieving this integration poses several challenges that must be addressed through innovative technological solutions and strategic regulatory frameworks.

One of the primary considerations for integrating CBDCs with existing financial systems is ensuring interoperability. Interoperability refers to the ability of different systems and technologies to work together seamlessly. For CBDCs, this means being able to interact with traditional banking systems, payment platforms, and other financial technologies. Achieving interoperability requires the development of common standards and protocols that enable CBDCs to be used alongside existing forms of money. This includes ensuring that CBDCs can be easily exchanged for fiat currency and other digital assets without friction.

The role of Application Programming Interfaces (APIs) is

crucial in enabling interoperability between CBDCs and existing financial systems. APIs allow different software applications to communicate with each other, facilitating the integration of CBDC functionality into banking apps, payment gateways, and other financial services platforms. By providing standardized APIs, central banks can enable financial institutions and fintech companies to incorporate CBDCs into their offerings, thereby expanding the usability and reach of digital currencies.

A significant aspect of integrating CBDCs is ensuring that they can coexist with existing payment methods, such as cash, credit cards, and electronic transfers. This coexistence is essential for providing users with a seamless payment experience and ensuring that the transition to digital currencies does not exclude individuals who may still rely on traditional payment methods. Hybrid systems that support both CBDCs and existing payment methods can help bridge the gap and facilitate a gradual transition to a more digital economy. These hybrid systems can be designed to automatically convert CBDCs to fiat currency and vice versa, allowing users to make payments using their preferred method.

Another critical factor in integrating CBDCs is the role of commercial banks. Commercial banks play a vital role in the financial system by providing banking services, facilitating payments, and extending credit. The introduction of CBDCs should not undermine the role of commercial banks but rather enhance their ability to serve customers. One approach to achieving this is through a two-tiered system where the central bank issues the CBDC, and commercial banks distribute it to the public. In this model, commercial banks would continue to manage customer accounts and provide traditional banking services while integrating CBDC functionalities into their operations. This approach ensures that commercial banks remain an integral part of the financial system while leveraging the benefits of digital currencies.

Payment infrastructure modernization is another area that requires attention for the successful integration of CBDCs. Many existing payment systems were designed decades ago and may not be equipped to handle the demands of modern digital currencies. Upgrading these systems to support real-time processing, enhanced security, and higher transaction volumes is essential. Blockchain and Distributed Ledger Technology (DLT) can play a significant role in this modernization effort. By leveraging the transparency, security, and efficiency of blockchain, central banks and financial institutions can create more robust and resilient payment infrastructures that support CBDCs.

Regulatory alignment is also crucial for the integration of CBDCs with existing financial systems. Regulatory frameworks must be updated to accommodate the unique characteristics of digital currencies while ensuring that they adhere to existing financial regulations. This includes addressing issues such as anti-money laundering (AML), counter-terrorism financing (CTF), data privacy, and consumer protection. Clear and consistent regulatory guidelines will provide financial institutions with the confidence to adopt and integrate CBDCs into their operations. Regulatory sandboxes, where new technologies and business models can be tested in a controlled environment, can be useful tools for developing and refining these guidelines.

Another important consideration is the impact of CBDCs on monetary policy and financial stability. The introduction of CBDCs has the potential to enhance the effectiveness of monetary policy by providing central banks with new tools for managing the money supply and interest rates. For example, CBDCs could enable more precise and timely implementation of monetary policy measures, such as adjusting interest rates directly on digital currency holdings. However, central banks must carefully consider the implications of CBDCs on financial stability, particularly in terms of their impact on commercial banks' deposit base and lending activities. A well-designed CBDC system should support the overall stability of the financial system and complement existing monetary policy tools.

Public trust and acceptance are essential for the successful integration of CBDCs. Building trust requires transparent communication about the benefits and risks of digital currencies, as well as clear guidelines on their use. Central banks and financial institutions must work together to educate the public about CBDCs, addressing concerns related to security, privacy, and the potential for financial exclusion. Ensuring that CBDCs are designed with user-friendly interfaces and accessible to all segments of the population, including those without access to traditional banking services, will be critical for their widespread adoption.

International cooperation is another key factor in the integration of CBDCs with existing financial systems. Given the global nature of financial markets, cross-border interoperability of CBDCs is essential for facilitating international trade and payments. Central banks and regulatory bodies must collaborate to develop common standards and protocols that enable CBDCs to function seamlessly across different jurisdictions. This cooperation will help prevent regulatory arbitrage and ensure that the global financial system remains stable and efficient.

The integration of Central Bank Digital Currencies with existing financial systems is a complex but essential task that requires careful planning, innovative technological solutions, and strategic regulatory frameworks. Achieving interoperability, modernizing payment infrastructure, aligning regulatory frameworks, and ensuring public trust are critical components of this integration process. By addressing these challenges, central banks can leverage the benefits of CBDCs to create a more efficient, inclusive, and resilient financial system that meets the evolving needs of the digital economy. The successful integration of CBDCs will ultimately depend on the collaborative efforts of central banks, financial institutions, regulatory bodies, and technology providers to create a cohesive and harmonious financial ecosystem.

CHAPTER 10:
ETHICAL AND SOCIAL
CONSIDERATIONS

10.1 Privacy Concerns and Data Protection in CBDCs

The adoption of Central Bank Digital Currencies (CBDCs) brings forth a myriad of ethical and social considerations, among which privacy concerns and data protection stand as paramount. As CBDCs integrate into the financial ecosystem, the balance between ensuring robust security and preserving individual privacy becomes increasingly intricate. This chapter delves into the critical issues surrounding privacy and data protection in the context of CBDCs, exploring the challenges, potential solutions, and the ethical imperatives that underpin these considerations.

Privacy in the realm of digital currencies is a double-edged sword. On one hand, the digital nature of CBDCs offers unprecedented transparency in financial transactions, which can significantly enhance the ability to monitor and prevent illicit activities such as money laundering, terrorism financing, and tax evasion. On the other hand, this transparency raises substantial concerns about the potential erosion of individual privacy. Unlike cash transactions, which are inherently private and leave no digital footprint, CBDC transactions are recorded on a digital ledger, potentially exposing sensitive financial information to a wider array of actors, including central banks, regulatory bodies, and potentially unauthorized third parties.

One of the primary concerns regarding CBDCs is the extent of data collection and the entities that have access to this data. Central banks, tasked with issuing and regulating CBDCs, will have unprecedented visibility into the financial transactions of individuals and businesses. This visibility can be a powerful tool for regulatory oversight and economic analysis, but it also raises significant privacy concerns. The centralization of vast amounts of financial data in the hands of a single institution can lead to the risk of misuse, whether through intentional surveillance, data breaches, or unauthorized access. The challenge lies in designing a CBDC system that provides necessary regulatory oversight while protecting the privacy of users.

Data protection in the context of CBDCs involves several critical components, including data minimization, secure data storage, and stringent access controls. Data minimization refers to the principle of collecting only the data that is necessary for a specific purpose and retaining it only for as long as necessary. In the case of CBDCs, this means that transaction data should be collected and stored in a way that is proportional to the needs of regulatory oversight and compliance without unnecessarily exposing personal financial details. Implementing robust encryption techniques and secure data storage solutions is essential to protect this data from breaches and unauthorized access.

The role of encryption in protecting privacy in CBDC transactions cannot be overstated. Advanced cryptographic techniques, such as zero-knowledge proofs (ZKPs) and homomorphic encryption, offer promising solutions for balancing transparency and privacy. ZKPs allow one party to prove to another that a statement is true without revealing any additional information. In the context of CBDCs, this means that transaction validity can be verified without disclosing the transaction details. Homomorphic encryption enables computations to be performed on encrypted data without decrypting it, allowing for data processing and analysis while maintaining privacy. These technologies can help ensure that sensitive financial information remains confidential while enabling necessary regulatory functions.

Another critical aspect of data protection in CBDCs is establishing clear and transparent governance frameworks for data access and usage. This involves defining who has access to transaction data, under what circumstances, and for what purposes. Central banks and regulatory authorities must implement stringent access controls and audit mechanisms to ensure that data is accessed and used only by authorized individuals and for legitimate purposes. Transparency in data governance can help build public trust and confidence in the CBDC system, reassuring users that their financial information is being handled responsibly and ethically.

The ethical considerations surrounding privacy and data protection in CBDCs extend beyond technological solutions to encompass broader societal implications. The potential for CBDCs to enable mass surveillance and infringe on individual freedoms is a significant ethical concern. In designing and implementing CBDCs, central banks and policymakers must consider the impact on civil liberties and strive to uphold the principles of privacy and autonomy. This includes engaging with stakeholders, including civil society organizations, privacy advocates, and the general public, to ensure that the design and governance of CBDCs align with societal values and expectations.

Another important ethical consideration is ensuring equitable access to privacy protections. In many cases, vulnerable populations, including low-income individuals and marginalized communities, are disproportionately affected by privacy violations and data misuse. CBDCs must be designed to provide robust privacy protections for all users, regardless of their socioeconomic status. This includes ensuring that privacy-enhancing technologies and practices are accessible and understandable to all segments of the population, not just those with advanced technological literacy.

The global nature of CBDCs also raises cross-border privacy and data protection challenges. As CBDCs facilitate international transactions, the regulatory frameworks and data protection standards of different jurisdictions come into play. Harmonizing these standards and ensuring cross-border data protection is a complex but essential task. International cooperation and agreements will be necessary to establish common principles and practices for data protection in CBDC transactions, ensuring that privacy is upheld regardless of where the transaction takes place.

Education and awareness are crucial components of addressing privacy concerns and data protection in CBDCs. Users must be informed about their rights and the measures in place to protect their privacy. Central banks and financial institutions should conduct public education campaigns to raise awareness about the importance of data protection and the specific protections offered by CBDCs. Empowering users with knowledge can help them make informed decisions and take proactive steps to protect their financial information.

Finally, continuous monitoring and improvement of privacy and data protection measures are essential to address evolving threats and challenges. The landscape of digital security is constantly changing, with new vulnerabilities and attack vectors emerging regularly. Central banks and regulatory authorities must remain vigilant and adaptive, regularly reviewing and updating their data protection practices to ensure they remain effective. This includes conducting regular security audits, staying abreast of technological advancements, and fostering a culture of continuous improvement.

Ensuring privacy and data protection in the implementation of Central Bank Digital Currencies requires a combination of advanced technological solutions, robust governance frameworks, and ethical considerations. By addressing these challenges holistically and engaging with stakeholders, central banks can create CBDC systems that protect individual privacy, enhance data security, and align with societal values and expectations. Through careful design and ongoing vigilance, CBDCs can offer the benefits of digital currencies while upholding the fundamental principles of privacy and data protection.

10.2 Economic Equality and Financial Inclusion with CBDCs

The advent of Central Bank Digital Currencies (CBDCs) presents a unique opportunity to address some of the persistent issues of economic inequality and financial exclusion that plague many societies around the world. CBDCs have the potential to democratize access to financial services, reduce transaction costs, and provide secure and efficient means of payment to underserved populations. This section explores how CBDCs can be leveraged to promote economic equality and financial inclusion, the challenges that must be overcome, and the ethical considerations involved in their deployment.

Financial inclusion refers to the availability and equality of opportunities to access financial services. In many parts of the world, significant portions of the population remain unbanked or underbanked, lacking access to basic financial services such as bank accounts, credit, and insurance. This exclusion hampers economic development and perpetuates poverty by limiting individuals' ability to save, invest, and manage financial risks. CBDCs can play a crucial role in bridging this gap by providing a digital alternative to traditional banking that is accessible to everyone with a smartphone or digital device.

One of the primary ways CBDCs can enhance financial inclusion is by lowering the barriers to accessing financial services. Traditional banking systems often require extensive documentation and credit history, which many low-income individuals and those in the informal economy do not possess. CBDCs, issued and managed by central banks, can be designed to require minimal documentation, making it easier for people to open digital wallets and start using digital currencies. This ease of access can be particularly beneficial in rural and remote areas where banking infrastructure is limited.

Moreover, CBDCs can significantly reduce transaction costs, which disproportionately affect the poor. Traditional financial transactions often involve high fees, especially for cross-border remittances, which are a lifeline for many families in developing countries. CBDCs, by enabling direct peer-to-peer transactions and reducing the need for intermediaries, can lower these costs, making financial transactions more affordable. Lower transaction costs can increase the disposable income of low-income households, enabling them to spend more on essential goods and services and invest in opportunities for economic advancement.

CBDCs can also provide a safer and more efficient means of payment, which is critical for financial inclusion. In many developing countries, cash remains the predominant form of payment, which can be insecure and inefficient. Carrying and storing cash poses significant risks, including theft and loss, and cash transactions lack transparency, making it difficult to build a credit history or access formal financial services. CBDCs offer a secure digital alternative that can reduce these risks and provide a traceable record of transactions, helping individuals build a financial history that can facilitate access to credit and other financial products.

The potential of CBDCs to enhance financial inclusion extends to the realm of government payments and social benefits. Governments can use CBDCs to distribute social welfare payments, subsidies, and emergency relief funds directly to beneficiaries' digital wallets. This direct distribution can ensure that financial assistance reaches those who need it most, without the delays and leakages often associated with traditional disbursement methods. By leveraging CBDCs, governments can improve the efficiency and transparency of social benefit programs, ensuring that public funds are used effectively to support vulnerable populations.

In addition to improving access to financial services and reducing costs, CBDCs can promote financial literacy and digital inclusion. Implementing CBDCs provides an opportunity to educate individuals about digital finance, helping them understand and utilize digital financial tools effectively. Financial literacy programs can be integrated into the rollout of CBDCs, providing training and resources to help people navigate the digital financial ecosystem. Increasing financial literacy can empower individuals to make informed financial decisions, improving their economic well-being and resilience.

Despite their potential benefits, the implementation of CBDCs for financial inclusion is not without challenges. One of the primary challenges is ensuring that the technological infrastructure necessary for CBDCs is available and accessible to everyone. This includes providing reliable internet connectivity and affordable digital devices, which are prerequisites for accessing and using digital currencies. Governments and central banks must work to address the digital divide by investing in digital infrastructure and ensuring that underserved communities have the tools and resources they need to participate in the digital economy.

Another challenge is designing CBDCs that are user-friendly

and accessible to people with varying levels of digital literacy. The user interfaces for CBDC wallets and applications must be intuitive and easy to navigate, even for individuals with limited experience with digital technologies. This requires thoughtful design and extensive user testing to ensure that CBDCs can be used effectively by everyone, including the elderly, people with disabilities, and those with limited education.

Privacy and security are also critical considerations in the deployment of CBDCs for financial inclusion. Ensuring that users' financial data is protected and that transactions are secure is essential for building trust in the digital currency system. Central banks must implement robust data protection measures and cybersecurity protocols to safeguard users' information and prevent fraud and cyberattacks. Additionally, clear and transparent communication about privacy protections and security measures can help build public confidence in CBDCs.

The ethical considerations of using CBDCs for financial inclusion also extend to the potential impact on existing financial institutions and services. While CBDCs can enhance access to financial services, they may also disrupt traditional banking models and pose challenges for commercial banks. Central banks must carefully consider the implications of CBDCs on the broader financial ecosystem and work to ensure that the introduction of digital currencies complements rather than undermines existing financial services. This may involve collaborating with commercial banks and fintech companies to integrate CBDCs into the financial system in a way that benefits all stakeholders.

Moreover, the deployment of CBDCs for financial inclusion must be accompanied by regulatory frameworks that protect consumers and ensure fair and equitable access to financial services. This includes establishing regulations that prevent discriminatory practices and ensure that CBDCs are accessible to all individuals, regardless of their socioeconomic status or geographic location. Regulatory oversight is also necessary to ensure that the benefits of CBDCs are distributed equitably and that the risks are managed effectively.

The global nature of CBDCs also requires international cooperation and coordination to address cross-border issues and ensure that digital currencies contribute to financial inclusion on a global scale. Central banks, governments, and international organizations must collaborate to develop common standards and best practices for the implementation of CBDCs, particularly in the context of cross-border transactions and remittances. International cooperation can help ensure that CBDCs are used to promote financial inclusion and economic equality across different regions and countries.

CBDCs have the potential to significantly enhance economic equality and financial inclusion by providing accessible, affordable, and secure financial services to underserved populations. However, realizing this potential requires addressing challenges related to technological infrastructure, user accessibility, privacy and security, and regulatory oversight. By leveraging CBDCs thoughtfully and ethically, central banks and governments can create a more inclusive financial system that empowers individuals, supports economic development, and promotes social equity.

10.3 Addressing the Digital Divide: Accessibility of CBDCs

The implementation of Central Bank Digital Currencies (CBDCs) offers a significant opportunity to enhance financial inclusion and economic equality. However, to fully realize this potential, it is crucial to address the digital divide, ensuring that CBDCs are accessible to all segments of the population, including those who are currently underserved by the financial system. The digital divide refers to the gap between individuals who have access to modern information and communication technology (ICT) and those who do not. Bridging this gap is essential for the successful adoption and utilization of CBDCs, as it will determine whether these digital currencies can truly democratize access to financial services.

One of the primary factors contributing to the digital divide is the lack of access to reliable internet connectivity. In many parts of the world, especially in rural and remote areas, internet infrastructure is underdeveloped or non-existent. This lack of connectivity poses a significant barrier to accessing digital financial services, including CBDCs. To overcome this challenge, governments and central banks must invest in expanding internet infrastructure, particularly in underserved regions. This investment can involve deploying broadband networks, satellite internet, and other innovative solutions to ensure that all individuals have access to reliable and affordable internet connectivity.

Affordable access to digital devices is another critical component of addressing the digital divide. Smartphones, tablets, and computers are essential tools for accessing and using CBDCs. However, the high cost of these devices can be prohibitive for low-income individuals and families. To make CBDCs accessible to a broader population, it is essential to promote the affordability of digital devices. This can be achieved through various measures, such as subsidizing the cost of devices, providing low-interest loans for purchasing digital equipment, and promoting the development and distribution of low-cost, high-quality devices. By making digital devices more affordable, governments can ensure that more people have the tools they need to participate in the digital economy.

Digital literacy is another crucial factor in bridging the digital divide. Even if individuals have access to internet connectivity and digital devices, they must possess the necessary skills and knowledge to use these technologies effectively. Digital literacy encompasses a range of competencies, including the ability to navigate digital interfaces, understand online security and privacy practices, and utilize digital financial tools. To enhance digital literacy, governments, central banks, and educational institutions should implement comprehensive digital education programs. These programs can include formal education in schools, community workshops, and online courses that teach individuals how to use digital technologies safely and effectively. By improving digital literacy, more people can confidently engage with CBDCs and other digital financial services.

In addition to expanding access to technology and improving digital literacy, it is essential to design CBDC systems that are user-friendly and accessible to individuals with varying levels of digital proficiency. This involves creating intuitive and straightforward interfaces that are easy to navigate, even for those who may not be technologically savvy. User-centered design principles should guide the development of CBDC wallets and applications, ensuring that they are inclusive and accessible to all users, including the elderly, people with disabilities, and those with limited education. Providing multiple language options and incorporating assistive technologies, such as screen readers and voice commands, can further enhance the accessibility of CBDCs.

Collaboration with local communities and organizations is also vital for addressing the digital divide. Community-based organizations, non-profits, and local governments can play a crucial role in reaching underserved populations and providing the necessary support and resources for adopting digital financial services. These organizations can help identify specific barriers to access within their communities and develop targeted interventions to address them. By working closely with local stakeholders, central banks and governments can ensure that their efforts to promote CBDCs are responsive to the unique needs and circumstances of different populations.

Privacy and security concerns are additional factors that can influence the accessibility of CBDCs. Individuals who are unfamiliar with digital technologies may be particularly wary of the risks associated with online financial transactions, such as fraud, identity theft, and data breaches. To build trust and encourage adoption, it is essential to implement robust security measures and communicate these measures clearly to users. This includes employing advanced encryption technologies, ensuring secure authentication processes, and regularly updating systems to protect against emerging threats. Transparent communication about privacy protections and security protocols can help alleviate concerns and build confidence in the safety of CBDCs.

Regulatory frameworks also play a critical role in ensuring the accessibility of CBDCs. Clear and consistent regulations can provide a stable environment for the development and deployment of digital currencies, ensuring that they are accessible and equitable. Regulations should address issues such as consumer protection, data privacy, and anti-discrimination to ensure that all individuals can access and benefit from CBDCs without facing undue barriers. Regulatory sandboxes, which allow for the testing of new technologies and business models in a controlled environment, can be valuable tools for developing and refining inclusive CBDC solutions.

International cooperation is another important aspect of addressing the digital divide. The challenges of digital exclusion are not confined to individual countries but are a global issue that requires coordinated efforts. International organizations, such as the United Nations, the World Bank, and the International Monetary Fund, can play a pivotal role in promoting digital inclusion by providing funding, expertise, and support for initiatives aimed at expanding access to technology and financial services. By working together, countries can share best practices, pool resources, and develop common standards and frameworks that promote the accessibility of CBDCs on a global scale.

Finally, ongoing monitoring and evaluation are essential for ensuring that efforts to address the digital divide are effective and responsive to changing circumstances. Governments and central banks should establish mechanisms for regularly assessing the impact of their initiatives, identifying areas for improvement, and making necessary adjustments. This continuous feedback loop can help ensure that strategies for promoting the accessibility of CBDCs remain relevant and effective in the face of evolving technological and social landscapes.

Addressing the digital divide is a multifaceted challenge that requires a holistic approach. By investing in internet infrastructure, promoting the affordability of digital devices, enhancing digital literacy, designing user-friendly CBDC systems, collaborating with local communities, implementing robust privacy and security measures, developing supportive regulatory frameworks, fostering international cooperation, and maintaining ongoing monitoring and evaluation, central banks and governments can ensure that CBDCs are accessible to all individuals. By bridging the digital divide, CBDCs can fulfill their potential to enhance financial inclusion and economic equality, providing secure, efficient, and inclusive financial services for everyone.

10.4 Ethical Implications of Digital Finance

The rise of digital finance, particularly with the advent of Central Bank Digital Currencies (CBDCs), brings forth a spectrum of ethical implications that must be carefully considered by policymakers, financial institutions, and society as a whole. While digital finance offers numerous benefits, such as increased efficiency, enhanced financial inclusion, and improved transaction security, it also poses significant ethical challenges that must be addressed to ensure that these technologies are used responsibly and equitably. This section delves into the ethical implications of digital finance, examining issues such as privacy, security, financial sovereignty, inequality, and the potential for misuse.

One of the most pressing ethical concerns in the realm of digital finance is the issue of privacy. Digital transactions inherently generate vast amounts of data, including sensitive personal and financial information. The collection, storage, and use of this data by central banks and other financial institutions raise significant privacy concerns. There is a delicate balance to be struck between leveraging data for legitimate purposes, such as improving financial services and ensuring regulatory compliance, and protecting individuals' privacy rights. Ethical considerations demand that robust data protection measures be implemented to safeguard individuals' privacy. This includes using advanced encryption techniques, ensuring data minimization, and establishing clear and transparent data governance frameworks that define who has access to data and under what circumstances.

Security is another critical ethical consideration in digital finance. The digital nature of CBDCs and other digital financial services makes them susceptible to cyber threats, including hacking, fraud, and identity theft. Ensuring the security of digital financial systems is essential to protect users' assets and maintain trust in the financial system. Ethical practices in digital finance require the implementation of stringent cybersecurity measures, continuous monitoring for potential threats, and rapid response mechanisms to address security breaches. Additionally, financial institutions must be transparent about the security measures in place and educate users on how to protect themselves from cyber threats.

Financial sovereignty is a fundamental ethical concern that arises with the introduction of CBDCs. Central banks and governments gain unprecedented control over individuals' financial transactions with CBDCs, raising questions about the potential for misuse of power. There is a risk that governments could use CBDCs to monitor and control individuals' financial activities, infringing on personal freedoms and autonomy. Ethical considerations necessitate that safeguards be put in place to prevent the abuse of this power. This includes establishing legal frameworks that protect individuals' rights and freedoms, ensuring that the use of CBDCs is transparent and accountable, and promoting public trust through open dialogue and engagement with stakeholders.

Inequality is another significant ethical issue in digital finance. While CBDCs have the potential to enhance financial inclusion and reduce inequality, there is also a risk that they could exacerbate existing disparities. Access to digital financial services requires reliable internet connectivity, digital devices, and digital literacy, which are not equally distributed across all populations. Ensuring that the benefits of CBDCs are equitably distributed requires addressing the digital divide, investing in digital infrastructure, and providing education and support to underserved communities. Ethical practices in digital finance demand a commitment to inclusivity, ensuring that no one is left behind in the transition to digital currencies.

The potential for misuse is an inherent ethical concern in digital finance. The same features that make CBDCs and other digital financial services efficient and powerful can also be exploited for illicit activities, such as money laundering, terrorism financing, and fraud. Ethical considerations require that robust mechanisms be implemented to detect and prevent the misuse of digital financial services. This includes adopting advanced technologies for monitoring and compliance, collaborating with international organizations to combat cross-border financial crimes, and ensuring that regulatory frameworks are adaptive and responsive to emerging threats.

Transparency is a key ethical principle that must underpin digital finance. The design, implementation, and operation of CBDCs and other digital financial services should be transparent to ensure public trust and accountability. This includes clear communication about how digital currencies work, the benefits and risks involved, and the measures in place to protect users. Transparency also involves engaging with stakeholders, including the public, to gather input and address concerns. By fostering an open and transparent environment, financial institutions can build trust and ensure that digital finance serves the public good.

Ethical considerations in digital finance also extend to the broader societal impacts of these technologies. The introduction of CBDCs and other digital financial services has the potential to disrupt traditional financial institutions and markets, leading to job displacement and economic shifts. Ethical practices require that these broader impacts be carefully considered and managed. This includes providing support and retraining for workers affected by technological change, ensuring that small businesses and vulnerable populations are not disproportionately impacted, and promoting policies that foster economic stability and resilience.

The role of international cooperation is crucial in addressing the ethical implications of digital finance. As digital currencies and financial services operate on a global scale, international collaboration is necessary to develop common standards, share best practices, and address cross-border ethical issues. This cooperation can help ensure that digital finance is developed and implemented in a way that upholds ethical principles and promotes the common good.

Education and awareness are vital components of addressing the ethical implications of digital finance. Users must be informed about their rights, the potential risks, and the ethical considerations involved in using digital financial services. Financial institutions and central banks should invest in educational programs that raise awareness about digital finance and empower users to make informed decisions. By promoting digital literacy and ethical awareness, society can ensure that digital finance is used responsibly and equitably.

In addressing the ethical implications of digital finance, it is essential to adopt a holistic and proactive approach. This involves integrating ethical considerations into the design and implementation of digital financial systems, continuously monitoring and evaluating the impacts, and engaging with stakeholders to address concerns and gather feedback. By prioritizing ethical principles, financial institutions and policymakers can ensure that digital finance contributes to a more just, equitable, and sustainable financial system.

The ethical implications of digital finance include issues of privacy, security, financial sovereignty, inequality, misuse, transparency, and broader societal impacts. Addressing these ethical challenges requires a commitment to robust data protection, cybersecurity, legal safeguards, inclusivity, transparency, international cooperation, and education. By upholding ethical principles and engaging with stakeholders, central banks and financial institutions can ensure that digital finance serves the public good and contributes to a more equitable and sustainable future.

CHAPTER 11:
FUTURE TRENDS
AND PREDICTIONS

11.1 The Evolution of Global Financial Markets with CBDCs

The introduction of Central Bank Digital Currencies (CBDCs) is poised to significantly alter the landscape of global financial markets. As countries worldwide explore and implement their digital currencies, the ripple effects on international finance, monetary policy, and economic structures will be profound. This chapter examines how CBDCs are expected to evolve global financial markets, highlighting potential trends, challenges, and transformative impacts.

The integration of CBDCs into global financial markets is likely to enhance the efficiency and transparency of financial transactions. Traditional financial systems often suffer from inefficiencies due to the involvement of multiple intermediaries, leading to delays and increased transaction costs. CBDCs, by leveraging advanced digital technologies, can streamline these processes. Digital currencies enable direct peer-to-peer transactions, reducing the need for intermediaries and thereby lowering transaction costs and settlement times. This efficiency is particularly beneficial for cross-border transactions, which are currently hindered by complex regulatory and operational barriers. With CBDCs, international payments can be executed more swiftly and at lower costs, fostering greater global trade and economic integration.

Another significant impact of CBDCs on global financial markets will be the enhancement of monetary policy tools available to central banks. Traditional monetary policy instruments, such as interest rate adjustments and open market operations, often have delayed and sometimes unpredictable effects on the economy. CBDCs offer central banks more direct and immediate mechanisms to influence the money supply and economic activity. For instance, central banks could implement programmable monetary policies, such as direct adjustments to interest rates on digital currency holdings or conditional transfers based on economic indicators. This capability can lead to more precise and effective monetary policy interventions, helping to stabilize economies and promote sustainable growth.

The widespread adoption of CBDCs also has the potential to reduce the dominance of the US dollar and other major currencies in global trade and finance. Currently, the US dollar is the primary currency for international transactions, which grants the United States significant economic influence. As more countries develop their own digital currencies, the reliance on the US dollar may diminish, leading to a more multipolar currency system. This shift could democratize international finance, giving smaller economies greater leverage and reducing the geopolitical influence of dominant currencies. However, this transition will require robust frameworks for currency interoperability and international regulatory cooperation to ensure stability and prevent fragmentation.

Financial inclusion is another area where CBDCs are expected to make a substantial impact. Despite advancements in financial technology, a significant portion of the global population remains unbanked or underbanked. CBDCs can provide a more accessible and inclusive financial ecosystem, allowing individuals without traditional bank accounts to participate in the digital economy. By offering a government-backed digital currency accessible through smartphones and other digital devices, central banks can extend financial services to remote and underserved areas. This inclusivity can drive economic growth by enabling more people to save, invest, and engage in commerce, thus lifting many out of poverty.

The introduction of CBDCs will also necessitate significant changes in the regulatory landscape. Existing financial regulations are primarily designed for traditional banking and financial systems. The advent of digital currencies requires a rethinking of these regulatory frameworks to address new challenges related to cybersecurity, privacy, and financial stability. Regulators will need to develop standards for digital currency issuance, transaction monitoring, and cross-border transfers. Additionally, there will be a need for enhanced international cooperation to harmonize regulations and prevent regulatory arbitrage, where entities exploit differences between jurisdictions to circumvent regulations.

The role of commercial banks in a CBDC-driven financial system will also evolve. While some fear that CBDCs could disintermediate traditional banks by allowing individuals to hold accounts directly with central banks, it is more likely that commercial banks will adapt to play new roles in the digital currency ecosystem. Commercial banks may become key facilitators of CBDC transactions, providing essential services such as digital wallet management, customer service, and compliance with regulatory requirements. Moreover, banks can leverage their expertise in financial services to develop innovative products and services that complement CBDCs, thereby enhancing their value proposition to customers.

Technological innovation will be a driving force in the evolution of global financial markets with CBDCs. Blockchain and distributed ledger technologies (DLT) will underpin many of the functionalities of digital currencies, providing secure, transparent, and efficient transaction mechanisms. Advances in cryptography, such as zero-knowledge proofs and homomorphic encryption, will enhance privacy and security, addressing concerns about data protection and transaction confidentiality. Furthermore, the integration of artificial intelligence (AI) and machine learning can improve the monitoring and analysis of financial transactions, aiding in the detection of fraud and the enforcement of regulatory compliance.

The evolution of global financial markets with CBDCs will also influence consumer behavior and societal norms. As digital currencies become more prevalent, individuals will likely become more accustomed to digital financial interactions, reducing the reliance on cash and traditional banking methods. This shift will necessitate increased digital literacy and financial education to ensure that all segments of society can navigate the new financial landscape effectively. Governments and educational institutions will play a crucial role in providing the necessary resources and training to prepare individuals for this transition.

The evolution of global financial markets with the introduction of Central Bank Digital Currencies will be transformative, affecting efficiency, monetary policy, financial inclusion, regulatory frameworks, the role of commercial banks, technological innovation, and consumer behavior. While the benefits are substantial, addressing the accompanying challenges will require coordinated efforts from central banks, financial institutions, regulators, and international organizations. As these stakeholders work together to shape the future of digital finance, the goal will be to create a more inclusive, efficient, and resilient global financial system that meets the needs of a rapidly changing world.

11.2 Central Banks' Long-Term
Strategies for Digital Currencies

As the financial landscape undergoes a digital transformation, central banks worldwide are developing long-term strategies to integrate Central Bank Digital Currencies (CBDCs) into their monetary systems. These strategies are designed to address the evolving needs of the economy, enhance financial stability, and ensure the effective implementation and management of digital currencies. This section explores the key elements of central banks' long-term strategies for CBDCs, including their objectives, the challenges they face, and the measures they are taking to overcome these challenges.

One of the primary objectives of central banks in developing CBDCs is to modernize the payment system. Traditional payment systems, which rely on physical currency and multiple intermediaries, can be slow, costly, and inefficient. By introducing CBDCs, central banks aim to create a more efficient and streamlined payment system that facilitates real-time transactions, reduces costs, and enhances the overall efficiency of the financial system. This modernization effort is particularly important in a global economy that increasingly relies on digital transactions and requires a robust infrastructure to support these activities.

Another key objective is to enhance financial inclusion. A significant portion of the global population remains unbanked or underbanked, lacking access to basic financial services. Central banks recognize that CBDCs can play a crucial role in providing these individuals with access to financial services. By offering a digital currency that can be easily accessed through smartphones and other digital devices, central banks can bring financial services to underserved and remote areas, promoting economic inclusion and empowerment. This objective aligns with broader social goals of reducing poverty and inequality by ensuring that all individuals have the tools they need to participate in the economy.

Ensuring the stability and security of the financial system is another critical objective for central banks. The introduction of CBDCs introduces new risks and challenges, including cybersecurity threats, potential disruptions to the banking sector, and the need for robust regulatory oversight. Central banks are developing comprehensive strategies to address these risks, which include implementing advanced cybersecurity measures, creating contingency plans for potential disruptions, and establishing clear regulatory frameworks to govern the use of digital currencies. These measures are designed to protect the financial system and maintain public trust in the integrity and security of CBDCs.

Central banks are also focused on maintaining monetary sovereignty and control over the monetary system. The rise of private digital currencies and stablecoins has the potential to undermine central banks' control over the money supply and monetary policy. By developing their own digital currencies, central banks can retain control over the monetary system, ensuring that they can effectively implement monetary policy and respond to economic challenges. This control is essential for maintaining economic stability and achieving macroeconomic objectives, such as controlling inflation, managing interest rates, and supporting economic growth.

To achieve these objectives, central banks are adopting a phased and iterative approach to the development and implementation of CBDCs. This approach allows them to test and refine the technology, address any issues that arise, and gradually scale up the deployment of digital currencies. Pilot programs and trials are a key component of this strategy, providing valuable insights into the practicalities of implementing CBDCs and allowing central banks to gather feedback from users and stakeholders.

These pilots help identify potential challenges and inform the development of policies and procedures to ensure the successful rollout of CBDCs.

Collaboration with stakeholders is another crucial element of central banks' long-term strategies for CBDCs. This collaboration includes working with commercial banks, fintech companies, technology providers, regulatory bodies, and international organizations. By engaging with a broad range of stakeholders, central banks can leverage their expertise, address diverse perspectives, and build a consensus around the design and implementation of CBDCs. This collaborative approach is essential for creating a digital currency ecosystem that is inclusive, secure, and effective.

Interoperability is a key consideration in the development of CBDCs. Central banks recognize that for digital currencies to be effective, they must be able to interact seamlessly with existing financial systems and other digital currencies. This requires the development of common standards and protocols that enable interoperability across different platforms and jurisdictions. By promoting interoperability, central banks can ensure that CBDCs can be used for a wide range of transactions, both domestically and internationally, enhancing their utility and adoption.

Education and public engagement are also important components of central banks' strategies for CBDCs. Ensuring that the public understands how digital currencies work, their benefits, and how to use them safely is essential for building trust and encouraging adoption. Central banks are investing in public education campaigns and providing resources to help individuals and businesses navigate the transition to digital currencies. This includes addressing concerns about privacy, security, and the impact of CBDCs on the broader financial system.

Regulatory and legal frameworks are being developed to support the implementation of CBDCs. Central banks are working with governments and regulatory bodies to create comprehensive policies that address issues such as data privacy, consumer protection, anti-money laundering (AML), and counter-terrorism financing (CTF). These frameworks are designed to ensure that CBDCs are used responsibly and ethically, protecting users and maintaining the integrity of the financial system. By establishing clear and consistent regulations, central banks can provide a stable environment for the development and use of digital currencies.

The role of international cooperation is increasingly important in the context of CBDCs. As digital currencies have the potential to impact global financial stability and economic integration, central banks are working with international organizations such as the International Monetary Fund (IMF), the Bank for International Settlements (BIS), and the Financial Stability Board (FSB) to develop common standards and best practices. This cooperation helps ensure that CBDCs are implemented in a way that supports global financial stability and facilitates cross-border transactions.

Finally, central banks are exploring the potential for CBDCs to support innovation and economic development. By creating a digital currency infrastructure, central banks can foster the development of new financial products and services, support the growth of fintech companies, and promote competition in the financial sector. This innovation can drive economic growth, create jobs, and enhance the overall competitiveness of the economy.

Central banks' long-term strategies for digital currencies are focused on modernizing payment systems, enhancing financial inclusion, ensuring stability and security, maintaining monetary sovereignty, and fostering innovation. These strategies involve a phased and iterative approach, collaboration with stakeholders, promoting interoperability, public education, regulatory frameworks, international cooperation, and support for innovation. By addressing these objectives and challenges, central banks can create a robust and effective framework for the development and implementation of CBDCs, ensuring that digital currencies contribute to a more efficient, inclusive, and resilient global financial system.

11.3 Potential Emergence of Global Digital Currencies

As the adoption of Central Bank Digital Currencies (CBDCs) accelerates, the financial world is increasingly contemplating the potential emergence of global digital currencies. These currencies could transform international trade, finance, and economic integration in profound ways. This section explores the prospects of global digital currencies, their potential benefits, challenges, and the implications for global economic dynamics.

Global digital currencies represent a natural evolution in a world where digital transactions and economic activities are becoming more interconnected. Unlike national CBDCs, which are issued and controlled by individual central banks, global digital currencies would be designed for use across multiple countries and regions. They could be issued by a consortium of central banks or international financial institutions, aiming to facilitate cross-border transactions, reduce currency exchange risks, and enhance global financial stability.

One of the primary drivers behind the push for global digital currencies is the need for more efficient and cost-effective cross-border payments. Currently, international transactions can be slow, expensive, and opaque due to the involvement of multiple intermediaries and varying regulatory environments. Global digital currencies could streamline these processes by providing a unified and interoperable platform for transactions. This would reduce transaction costs, increase transaction speed, and provide greater transparency, benefiting businesses, consumers, and financial institutions alike.

Another significant benefit of global digital currencies is the potential reduction in currency exchange risks. Businesses and individuals engaged in international trade and finance often face the uncertainty of fluctuating exchange rates, which can impact profitability and financial planning. A global digital currency, used as a common medium of exchange, could mitigate these risks by providing a stable and universally accepted currency. This stability would facilitate smoother international transactions and financial planning, fostering greater economic integration and cooperation.

The emergence of global digital currencies could also enhance financial inclusion on a global scale. Many individuals and businesses, particularly in developing countries, face barriers to accessing traditional banking services and international markets. Global digital currencies, accessible via digital platforms, could provide these underserved populations with easier access to financial services and global markets. This inclusivity could drive economic growth, reduce poverty, and promote equitable economic development worldwide.

However, the development and implementation of global digital currencies are fraught with challenges. One of the primary concerns is the governance and regulatory framework needed to support such currencies. A global digital currency would require robust and coordinated regulation to ensure its stability, security, and compliance with international laws. Establishing this framework involves significant cooperation among countries with diverse economic interests and regulatory environments. Ensuring that all participating countries adhere to common standards and practices is essential to the success of a global digital currency.

Another challenge is the potential impact on national sovereignty and monetary policy. Central banks use their control over national currencies as a tool for implementing monetary policy and managing their economies. The introduction of a global digital currency could limit the ability of central banks to influence their domestic economies, leading to concerns about the loss of monetary sovereignty. To address this, any global digital currency system must be designed to complement rather than replace national currencies, allowing central banks to retain control over their monetary policies while benefiting from the efficiencies of a global currency.

The issue of privacy and data protection is also critical in the context of global digital currencies. Ensuring the privacy and security of financial transactions is paramount to gaining public trust and acceptance. The digital nature of global currencies necessitates advanced cybersecurity measures and robust data protection frameworks to safeguard user information and prevent misuse. Balancing the need for transparency and regulatory oversight with the protection of individual privacy is a complex but essential task.

Technological infrastructure is another area that requires careful consideration. The successful implementation of a global digital currency depends on the availability of reliable and secure digital infrastructure. This includes ensuring that all participating countries have access to the necessary technology and that their systems are interoperable. Developing this infrastructure requires significant investment and international cooperation to address disparities in technological capabilities and resources.

The potential for geopolitical tensions also poses a challenge to the emergence of global digital currencies. Countries may have differing views on the governance and use of such currencies, leading to conflicts and disagreements. Navigating these geopolitical complexities requires diplomatic efforts and the establishment of international agreements that balance the interests of all parties involved.

Despite these challenges, several initiatives are already exploring the concept of global digital currencies. For example, the International Monetary Fund (IMF) and the Bank for International Settlements (BIS) have been conducting research and pilot projects to assess the feasibility and implications of digital currencies in a global context. These initiatives aim to develop frameworks and standards that could support the implementation of global digital currencies while addressing the associated challenges.

The potential emergence of global digital currencies also raises questions about the role of existing international reserve currencies, such as the US dollar and the euro. A widely adopted global digital currency could reduce the dominance of these reserve currencies, leading to shifts in global economic power and influence. This transition would require careful management to ensure stability and prevent economic disruptions.

The potential emergence of global digital currencies represents a significant development in the evolution of the global financial system. These currencies offer the promise of more efficient and inclusive international transactions, reduced currency exchange risks, and enhanced financial stability. However, realizing this potential requires overcoming substantial challenges related to governance, regulation, monetary sovereignty, privacy, technological infrastructure, and geopolitical tensions. As research and pilot projects continue to explore the feasibility of global digital currencies, international cooperation and coordination will be crucial to addressing these challenges and ensuring that these currencies contribute to a more efficient, stable, and inclusive global economy. The journey toward global digital currencies is complex, but with thoughtful planning and collaboration, it holds the promise of transforming the future of international finance.

11.4 Preparing for a Digitally Dominated Financial Future

As Central Bank Digital Currencies (CBDCs) and other digital financial innovations gain traction, the global financial landscape is on the cusp of a significant transformation. Preparing for a digitally dominated financial future requires comprehensive strategies that encompass technological readiness, regulatory frameworks, financial education, and international cooperation. This section explores the key steps that governments, financial institutions, businesses, and individuals must take to navigate and thrive in this evolving environment.

Central to preparing for a digitally dominated financial future is the development and implementation of robust technological infrastructure. Governments and financial institutions must invest in advanced technologies that support the seamless operation of digital currencies and digital financial services. This includes upgrading existing payment systems to handle real-time transactions, enhancing cybersecurity measures to protect against digital threats, and ensuring that all regions, including rural and underserved areas, have access to reliable internet connectivity and digital devices. Additionally, developing interoperable systems that allow different digital currencies and financial platforms to work together seamlessly is crucial for creating an inclusive and efficient digital financial ecosystem.

Regulatory frameworks must evolve to address the unique challenges and opportunities presented by digital finance. Policymakers need to establish clear, consistent, and adaptive regulations that ensure the stability and security of the financial system while fostering innovation. This involves creating standards for the issuance and management of digital currencies, implementing robust data protection and privacy laws, and developing mechanisms for monitoring and mitigating systemic risks. Regulatory sandboxes can play a vital role in this process, allowing financial institutions and fintech companies to test new technologies and business models in a controlled environment, providing valuable insights that inform regulatory development.

Financial education and digital literacy are critical components of preparing for a digitally dominated financial future. As digital currencies and financial technologies become more prevalent, individuals and businesses must be equipped with the knowledge and skills to use these tools effectively and safely. Governments, educational institutions, and financial organizations should collaborate to offer comprehensive financial education programs that cover the basics of digital finance, the benefits and risks of digital currencies, and best practices for cybersecurity and data protection. Empowering people with digital literacy will help ensure that they can participate fully in the digital economy, make informed financial decisions, and protect themselves from fraud and cyber threats.

International cooperation is essential for managing the global implications of digital finance. Digital currencies and financial technologies do not recognize national borders, making international coordination crucial for addressing cross-border issues such as regulatory arbitrage, money laundering, and cybersecurity. Central banks, governments, and international organizations must work together to develop harmonized standards and best practices that promote the secure and efficient use of digital finance globally. This cooperation can also facilitate the development of cross-border payment systems that reduce transaction costs and enhance financial inclusion for individuals and businesses engaged in international trade.

For businesses, preparing for a digitally dominated financial future involves adopting and integrating digital financial tools into their operations. This includes accepting digital currencies as a form of payment, leveraging blockchain technology for supply chain management and contract execution, and using advanced analytics to enhance financial planning and decision-making. Businesses should also invest in cybersecurity measures to protect against digital threats and ensure the privacy and security of customer data. By embracing digital finance, businesses can improve efficiency, reduce costs, and better serve their customers in a rapidly evolving market.

Financial institutions, particularly banks, must adapt their business models to remain relevant in a digital-first financial environment. This adaptation involves offering digital currency services, such as digital wallets and payment processing, and developing new financial products that leverage digital technologies. Banks should also focus on enhancing customer experience by providing seamless and secure digital banking services, personalized financial advice through artificial intelligence, and user-friendly interfaces. Collaboration with fintech companies can help banks accelerate their digital transformation and offer innovative solutions that meet the changing needs of their customers.

Individuals also have a role to play in preparing for a digitally dominated financial future. As consumers of financial services, individuals need to stay informed about the latest developments in digital finance and understand how to use digital currencies and financial tools safely and effectively. This includes practicing good cybersecurity hygiene, such as using strong passwords, enabling two-factor authentication, and being vigilant against phishing scams. Additionally, individuals should take advantage of financial education resources to enhance their digital literacy and make informed decisions about managing their finances in a digital world.

The potential benefits of a digitally dominated financial future are vast, including greater financial inclusion, increased efficiency, enhanced security, and new opportunities for innovation and economic growth. However, realizing these benefits requires addressing significant challenges and managing the risks associated with digital finance. Policymakers, financial institutions, businesses, and individuals must work together to create a financial ecosystem that is inclusive, secure, and resilient.

Preparation for a digitally dominated financial future encompasses technological readiness, regulatory adaptation, financial education, and international cooperation. By investing in advanced technologies, developing adaptive regulatory frameworks, promoting digital literacy, and fostering international collaboration, society can navigate the transition to a digital financial landscape effectively. This preparation will enable governments, businesses, financial institutions, and individuals to leverage the benefits of digital finance while mitigating the associated risks, ultimately contributing to a more efficient, inclusive, and dynamic global financial system.

EPILOGUE

Reflections on the Future of
Money and Global Finance

As we stand on the brink of a new era in global finance, the future of money is being reshaped by rapid technological advancements, shifting economic paradigms, and evolving societal needs. Central Bank Digital Currencies (CBDCs) represent a transformative innovation that promises to redefine how we understand and interact with money. The journey toward digital currencies and a digitally dominated financial future is fraught with challenges, but it also offers unparalleled opportunities to create a more inclusive, efficient, and resilient financial system.

The evolution of CBDCs and digital finance is not merely a technological shift; it is a fundamental rethinking of the roles and functions of money in our societies. Money has always been a cornerstone of economic activity, a store of value, a medium of exchange, and a unit of account. With the advent of digital currencies, these functions are being enhanced and expanded, offering new possibilities for how we conduct transactions, save, invest, and interact with the global economy.

One of the most profound impacts of CBDCs is their potential to enhance financial inclusion. By providing a secure, accessible, and affordable means of conducting financial transactions, CBDCs can bring millions of unbanked and underbanked individuals into the formal financial system. This inclusion can drive economic development, reduce poverty, and promote equitable growth. As digital financial services become more prevalent, they offer a pathway to financial empowerment for individuals and communities that have been historically marginalized.

The integration of CBDCs into the global financial system also promises to enhance efficiency and reduce transaction costs. Traditional payment systems, often burdened by intermediaries and complex regulatory environments, can be slow and expensive. CBDCs, leveraging blockchain and other advanced technologies, can streamline these processes, enabling faster and cheaper transactions both domestically and internationally. This increased efficiency can benefit businesses and consumers alike, fostering greater economic dynamism and competitiveness.

However, the transition to a digital financial future is not without its challenges. Ensuring the security and privacy of digital transactions is paramount. The digital nature of CBDCs makes them susceptible to cyber threats, requiring robust cybersecurity measures and continuous vigilance. Protecting the privacy of individuals while maintaining the transparency necessary for regulatory oversight presents a complex balancing act. These challenges must be addressed through advanced technological solutions, stringent regulatory frameworks, and a commitment to upholding ethical standards.

The regulatory landscape for digital currencies is still evolving, and it must adapt to the unique characteristics of digital finance. Policymakers must develop comprehensive and adaptive regulations that promote innovation while safeguarding financial stability and consumer protection. This involves international cooperation to harmonize standards and practices, ensuring that digital currencies can operate seamlessly across borders. Regulatory sandboxes and pilot programs can provide valuable insights into the practicalities of implementing digital currencies, helping to refine policies and address potential issues before widespread adoption.

The role of central banks is also evolving in this new financial paradigm. Central banks must navigate the delicate balance between fostering innovation and maintaining control over monetary policy and financial stability. By issuing and managing CBDCs, central banks can leverage new tools for monetary policy implementation, potentially enhancing their ability to respond to economic fluctuations and crises. However, this also requires careful consideration of the implications for commercial banks and the broader financial system.

Technological innovation will continue to drive the evolution of money and finance. Advances in blockchain, artificial intelligence, and cryptography will shape the capabilities and security of digital currencies. As these technologies mature, they will enable new applications and services that were previously unimaginable, further transforming the financial landscape. Financial institutions, fintech companies, and technology providers must collaborate to harness these innovations and create value for consumers and businesses.

The societal implications of a digital financial future are significant. As digital currencies become more integrated into everyday life, they will change how we think about and use money. Financial education and digital literacy will be crucial to ensuring that individuals can navigate this new landscape effectively and securely. Public trust in digital financial systems must be built and maintained through transparency, accountability, and a demonstrated commitment to protecting users' interests.

Reflecting on the future of money and global finance, it is clear that we are at a pivotal moment. The choices we make today in designing and implementing digital currencies will shape the financial systems of tomorrow. It is an opportunity to create a more inclusive, efficient, and resilient financial ecosystem that meets the needs of all people, regardless of their location or economic status. By embracing innovation while upholding ethical principles and ensuring robust regulatory oversight, we can navigate the challenges and unlock the full potential of digital finance.

In this transformative journey, collaboration and cooperation are essential. Governments, central banks, financial institutions, technology providers, and international organizations must work together to develop a shared vision for the future of money. This vision should prioritize the well-being of individuals and communities, promoting economic growth and stability while protecting privacy and security.

As we look to the future, it is important to remain adaptable and responsive to new developments and challenges. The financial landscape will continue to evolve, and we must be prepared to evolve with it. By fostering a culture of continuous learning, innovation, and ethical responsibility, we can ensure that the future of money and global finance is bright, inclusive, and sustainable.

The future of money is being shaped by the convergence of technological innovation, economic necessity, and societal change. CBDCs and digital finance offer unprecedented opportunities to transform the global financial system, making it more efficient, inclusive, and resilient. The path forward will require careful planning, robust regulation, and a commitment to ethical principles. By embracing these challenges and opportunities, we can build a financial future that benefits all of humanity, driving progress and prosperity for generations to come.

GLOSSARY

Key Terms and Concepts

Central Bank Digital Currency (CBDC): A digital form of a country's national currency issued and regulated by the central bank. Unlike cryptocurrencies, CBDCs are centralized and serve as legal tender, designed to complement or replace traditional physical currency.

Cryptocurrency: A decentralized digital or virtual currency that uses cryptography for security. Bitcoin, Ethereum, and Litecoin are examples of cryptocurrencies. Unlike CBDCs, cryptocurrencies are typically not issued or regulated by any central authority.

Blockchain: A decentralized digital ledger that records transactions across multiple computers in such a way that the registered transactions cannot be altered retroactively. Blockchain technology is the backbone of most cryptocurrencies and can be used for various applications, including supply chain management and smart contracts.

Distributed Ledger Technology (DLT): A digital system for recording the transaction of assets in which the transactions and their details are recorded in multiple places at the same time. Unlike traditional databases, distributed ledgers do not have a central data store or administrative functionality.

Smart Contracts: Self-executing contracts with the terms of the agreement directly written into code. They run on blockchain platforms and automatically enforce and execute the terms of the contract when predefined conditions are met.

Financial Inclusion: The process of ensuring access to appropriate, affordable, and timely financial products and services by all individuals and businesses, particularly those that are traditionally underserved or excluded from the financial system.

Interoperability: The ability of different systems, platforms, or networks to work together seamlessly. In the context of digital currencies, interoperability ensures that different CBDCs and digital financial services can interact and operate across various platforms and jurisdictions.

Decentralization: The distribution of power and control away from a central authority. In digital finance, decentralization often refers to systems where transactions and operations are managed across a distributed network of computers rather than a central entity.

Monetary Policy: The process by which a central bank manages the money supply and interest rates to achieve macroeconomic objectives such as controlling inflation, managing employment levels, and maintaining financial stability.

Peer-to-Peer (P2P) Transactions: Transactions that occur directly between two parties without the need for intermediaries. Digital currencies often facilitate P2P transactions, reducing the need for traditional banking intermediaries.

Digital Wallet: An electronic device or online service that allows individuals to make electronic transactions. A digital wallet can store digital currency, cryptocurrencies, and other payment information.

Anti-Money Laundering (AML): Laws, regulations, and procedures aimed at preventing criminals from disguising illegally obtained funds as legitimate income. AML measures are critical in the digital currency space to prevent financial crimes.

Know Your Customer (KYC): The process by which financial institutions verify the identity of their clients. KYC procedures are essential to comply with regulatory requirements and to prevent fraud and money laundering.

Proof of Work (PoW): A consensus mechanism used in blockchain networks to validate transactions and create new blocks. In PoW, participants (miners) solve complex mathematical problems, and the first to solve the problem gets to add the block to the blockchain and is rewarded with cryptocurrency.

Proof of Stake (PoS): An alternative to Proof of Work, PoS is a consensus mechanism where validators are chosen to create new blocks and validate transactions based on the number of coins they hold and are willing to "stake" as collateral.

Zero-Knowledge Proofs (ZKPs): Cryptographic methods that allow one party to prove to another that a statement is true without revealing any additional information. ZKPs can enhance privacy in digital transactions by allowing verification without disclosing transaction details.

Homomorphic Encryption: A form of encryption that allows computations to be performed on encrypted data without needing to decrypt it first. This technology can help maintain privacy while enabling data processing in digital financial systems.

Regulatory Sandbox: A framework set up by a regulatory body that allows fintech companies and other innovators to conduct live experiments in a controlled environment under a regulator's supervision. This helps in developing and testing new financial products and services while ensuring compliance with regulatory requirements.

Financial Stability: The condition in which the financial system

– including financial institutions, markets, and infrastructure – operates effectively, withstands shocks, and continues to support economic growth and development.

Digital Divide: The gap between individuals who have access to modern information and communication technology and those who do not. Addressing the digital divide is crucial for ensuring equitable access to digital financial services and the benefits of digital currencies.

Tokenization: The process of converting rights to an asset into a digital token on a blockchain. Tokenization can be applied to various assets, including real estate, stocks, and commodities, enabling fractional ownership and increased liquidity.

Cybersecurity: The practice of protecting systems, networks, and programs from digital attacks. In the context of digital currencies, robust cybersecurity measures are essential to prevent fraud, data breaches, and other cyber threats.

Liquidity: The ease with which an asset can be converted into cash without affecting its market price. High liquidity in financial markets is essential for smooth and efficient transactions.

Programmable Money: Digital money that can be programmed to perform specific functions based on predefined rules. CBDCs can be designed as programmable money, enabling automated and conditional transactions.

Monetary Sovereignty: The ability of a state to exercise control over its currency and monetary policy. The introduction of digital currencies raises questions about maintaining monetary sovereignty, particularly in the context of cross-border digital currencies.

Cross-Border Payments: Financial transactions where the payer and the recipient are located in different countries. Cross-border payments can be complex and costly, and digital currencies have the potential to streamline these transactions.

Fiat Currency: Government-issued currency that is not backed by a physical commodity but rather by the government that issued it. Examples include the US dollar, the euro, and the yen. Fiat currency contrasts with cryptocurrencies and CBDCs, which may or may not be government-issued.

Stablecoin: A type of cryptocurrency designed to minimize price volatility by being pegged to a stable asset, such as a fiat currency or a basket of goods. Stablecoins aim to combine the benefits of digital currencies with the stability of traditional currencies.

Digital Transformation: The integration of digital technology into all areas of business and society, fundamentally changing how organizations operate and deliver value to customers. In finance, digital transformation includes the adoption of digital currencies and financial technologies.

Token Economy: An economic system that uses digital tokens for transactions. Tokens can represent various assets and are used in blockchain ecosystems for trading, investing, and accessing services.

Legal Tender: Money that must be accepted if offered in payment of a debt. CBDCs are expected to be legal tender, just like traditional fiat currency, ensuring their acceptance for transactions and debt settlements.

International Monetary Fund (IMF): An international organization that aims to promote global monetary cooperation, secure financial stability, facilitate international trade, and reduce poverty. The IMF plays a role in the global discussion on digital currencies and financial stability.

Bank for International Settlements (BIS): An international financial institution that serves as a bank for central banks, fostering international monetary and financial cooperation and promoting financial stability. The BIS conducts research and provides insights into the implications of digital currencies.

Financial Technology (Fintech): Technology and innovation that aim to compete with traditional financial methods in the delivery of financial services. Fintech companies leverage technologies such as blockchain, AI, and big data to offer innovative financial solutions.

Central Bank: The institution responsible for managing a country's currency, money supply, and interest rates. Central banks also oversee the commercial banking system and implement monetary policy. Central banks are key players in the development and issuance of CBDCs.

Decentralized Finance (DeFi): A blockchain-based form of finance that does not rely on central financial intermediaries such as brokerages, exchanges, or banks. DeFi platforms allow people to lend, borrow, and trade directly with one another using smart contracts on blockchain networks.

Digital Twin: A virtual representation of a physical object or system that can be used to simulate, analyze, and optimize its real-world counterpart. In finance, digital twins can be used to model financial systems and predict the impact of changes or disruptions.

Open Banking: A financial services practice that provides third-party financial service providers open access to consumer banking, transaction, and other financial data through the use of application programming interfaces (APIs). Open banking aims to foster greater transparency, innovation, and competition in the financial services sector.

Monetary Sovereignty: The authority of a state to control its own currency and monetary policy. The advent of CBDCs challenges traditional notions of monetary sovereignty by introducing a digital form of national currency that may require new forms of governance and control.

Legal Frameworks: The set of laws and regulations that govern the issuance, distribution, and use of digital currencies. Legal frameworks for CBDCs must address issues such as data protection, anti-money laundering, consumer protection, and financial stability.

Cyber Resilience: The ability of an organization or system to withstand, recover from, and adapt to cyberattacks. In the context of CBDCs, cyber resilience is crucial to ensure the continuous and secure operation of digital currency systems.

Interbank Settlement: The process by which banks exchange payments to settle transactions between their customers. CBDCs have the potential to streamline interbank settlements, making them faster and more efficient.

Digital Identity: The online representation of an individual's or organization's identity. Digital identities are essential for verifying the identities of users in digital currency transactions, ensuring compliance with KYC and AML regulations.

Privacy Coins: Cryptocurrencies that prioritize user privacy and anonymity by obscuring transaction details. Examples include Monero and Zcash. Privacy coins raise important questions about the balance between privacy and regulatory compliance in the digital currency space.

Regulatory Arbitrage: The practice of taking advantage of differences in regulatory environments between jurisdictions. As CBDCs are implemented globally, preventing regulatory arbitrage requires harmonizing regulations across countries to ensure a level playing field.

Proof of Authority (PoA): A consensus mechanism used in blockchain networks where a limited number of validators are authorized to validate transactions and create new blocks. PoA provides higher transaction throughput and lower latency compared to PoW and PoS.

Fiat-Backed Stablecoin: A type of stablecoin that is backed by reserves of fiat currency, such as the US dollar or the euro. Fiat-backed stablecoins aim to provide the stability of traditional currencies with the benefits of digital assets.

Algorithmic Stablecoin: A type of stablecoin that uses algorithms to maintain its value. Unlike fiat-backed stablecoins, algorithmic stablecoins are not backed by physical reserves but rely on smart contracts to manage supply and demand dynamically.

Digital Assets: Any asset that exists in a digital form and has value. Digital assets include cryptocurrencies, CBDCs, digital securities, and tokens representing real-world assets such as real estate or commodities.

Quantum Computing: An emerging technology that leverages the principles of quantum mechanics to perform computations much faster than traditional computers. Quantum computing poses both opportunities and threats to digital currencies, particularly in the realm of cryptography.

Decentralized Autonomous Organization (DAO): An organization represented by rules encoded as a computer program that is transparent, controlled by organization members, and not influenced by a central government. DAOs operate on blockchain networks and enable decentralized governance and decision-making.

Consensus Mechanism: The method by which a blockchain network reaches agreement on the validity of transactions and the state of the ledger. Common consensus mechanisms include Proof of Work (PoW), Proof of Stake (PoS), and Proof of Authority (PoA).

Digital Ledger: A digital record of transactions maintained in a decentralized manner across multiple computers. Digital ledgers are the foundation of blockchain technology and provide transparency and security for digital currency transactions.

Programmable Transactions: Transactions that are executed automatically based on predefined conditions. Programmable transactions enable advanced financial applications such as automated payments, conditional transfers, and smart contracts.

Public Key Infrastructure (PKI): A framework for managing digital keys and certificates that enables secure and authenticated communication. PKI is essential for the security of digital currency transactions, providing a foundation for encryption and digital signatures.

Cross-Border Remittances: Money transfers from individuals in one country to recipients in another. Cross-border remittances are often costly and slow, but CBDCs and digital currencies have the potential to streamline these transactions and reduce costs.

Digital Transformation in Finance: The integration of digital technology into all aspects of financial services, fundamentally changing how financial institutions operate and deliver value to customers. This transformation includes the adoption of digital currencies, fintech innovations, and data analytics.

Digital Currency Issuance: The process by which a central bank or other authority creates and distributes digital currency. The issuance process involves technical, regulatory, and economic considerations to ensure the stability and acceptance of the digital currency.

Tokenized Assets: Assets that are represented by digital tokens on a blockchain. Tokenized assets can include anything from real estate to stocks, enabling fractional ownership and increased liquidity.

Secure Multiparty Computation (SMPC): A cryptographic protocol that allows multiple parties to jointly compute a function over their inputs while keeping those inputs private. SMPC can enhance the privacy and security of digital currency transactions.

Blockchain Interoperability: The ability of different blockchain networks to communicate and interact with each other. Interoperability is crucial for the widespread adoption of digital currencies, enabling seamless transactions across various platforms and ecosystems.

Financial Ecosystem: The network of financial institutions, markets, and infrastructures that facilitate financial transactions and services. The financial ecosystem is being transformed by digital currencies and fintech innovations, leading to new opportunities and challenges.

Digital Currency Adoption: The process by which individuals, businesses, and governments begin to use digital currencies for transactions and financial activities. Adoption is influenced by factors such as technological infrastructure, regulatory environment, and public trust.

Data Privacy in Digital Finance: The protection of personal and financial information in digital transactions. Ensuring data privacy is essential for maintaining trust in digital currencies and complying with legal and regulatory requirements.

Stable Value Assets: Assets designed to maintain a stable value over time, often used as a store of value in digital finance. Stablecoins and CBDCs can be considered stable value assets, providing stability in volatile markets.

Digital Currency Exchange: A platform that allows users to buy, sell, and trade digital currencies. Exchanges play a critical role in the digital currency ecosystem, providing liquidity and price discovery for digital assets.

Real-Time Gross Settlement (RTGS): A system that allows for the real-time settlement of transactions between banks. RTGS systems are being adapted to accommodate digital currencies, enabling faster and more efficient payment processing.

Cryptographic Hash Function: A mathematical algorithm that transforms input data into a fixed-size string of characters, which appears random. Hash functions are used in blockchain technology to secure data and ensure the integrity of transactions.

Public and Private Keys: Cryptographic keys used in digital finance to secure transactions. A public key is shared openly and used to encrypt data, while a private key is kept secret and used to decrypt data or sign transactions.

Digital Currency Ecosystem: The interconnected network of technologies, institutions, and users involved in the creation, distribution, and use of digital currencies. The ecosystem includes central banks, commercial banks, fintech companies, exchanges, and consumers.

Global Financial Integration: The process by which financial markets and institutions become interconnected and interdependent across borders. Digital currencies have the potential to enhance global financial integration by facilitating cross-border transactions and reducing barriers.

Digital Financial Inclusion: The effort to ensure that all individuals and businesses, particularly those in underserved or remote areas, have access to digital financial services. Digital financial inclusion aims to reduce inequality and promote economic development.

Central Bank Digital Wallet: A digital wallet issued by a central bank that allows individuals and businesses to store and use CBDCs. Central bank digital wallets provide a secure and accessible platform for managing digital currency holdings.

Digital Currency Pilots: Experimental programs conducted by central banks and financial institutions to test the feasibility and implications of digital currencies. Pilots provide valuable insights and inform the development of CBDC policies and systems.

Digital Currency Framework: The set of principles, policies, and technologies that guide the development and implementation of digital currencies. A robust framework ensures the stability, security, and acceptance of digital currencies.

Digital Currency Governance: The systems and processes that oversee the issuance, distribution, and use of digital currencies. Governance involves regulatory oversight, policy development, and stakeholder engagement to ensure the effective management of digital currencies.

Digital Payment Infrastructure: The network of technologies and systems that support digital currency transactions. This infrastructure includes payment gateways, digital wallets, blockchain networks, and cybersecurity measures.

Digital Currency Accessibility: The ease with which individuals and businesses can access and use digital currencies. Ensuring accessibility involves addressing technological, economic, and educational barriers to digital currency adoption.

Privacy Enhancing Technologies (PETs): Technologies designed to protect user privacy in digital transactions. PETs include encryption, zero-knowledge proofs, and secure multiparty computation, providing tools to ensure data privacy in digital finance.

Digital Currency Ecosystem Stakeholders: The various parties involved in the creation, distribution, and use of digital currencies. Stakeholders include central banks, commercial banks, fintech companies, regulatory bodies, technology providers, and consumers.

Monetary Policy Transmission: The process by which central bank actions, such as interest rate changes, influence economic activity. CBDCs offer new tools for monetary policy transmission, potentially enhancing the effectiveness of central bank interventions.

Cryptoeconomics: The study of the economic principles and incentives that drive the behavior of participants in blockchain and digital currency systems. Cryptoeconomics combines elements of cryptography, economics, and game theory to design secure and efficient digital currency protocols.

Tokenomics: The economic structure and principles underlying the use and distribution of tokens in a digital currency ecosystem. Tokenomics involves the study of supply and demand dynamics, token distribution models, and incentives for participation.

Digital Financial Stability: The resilience of the digital financial system to shocks and disruptions. Ensuring digital financial stability involves implementing robust regulatory frameworks, cybersecurity measures, and contingency plans to address potential risks.

Cross-Border Interoperability: The ability of digital currency systems to function seamlessly across

different countries and jurisdictions. Achieving cross-border interoperability requires harmonizing standards and regulations to facilitate international transactions.

Financial Ecosystem Disruption: The changes and challenges brought about by the introduction of digital currencies and fintech innovations. Disruption can lead to new opportunities and efficiencies, but also requires adaptation and risk management by financial institutions.

Digital Currency Adoption Curve: The progression of digital currency adoption over time, from early experimentation to widespread use. Understanding the adoption curve helps policymakers and financial institutions plan for the gradual integration of digital currencies into the financial system.

Central Bank Digital Currency (CBDC) Research: The study and analysis of the implications, benefits, and challenges of CBDCs. Research informs the development of CBDC policies and systems, ensuring that they meet the needs of the economy and society.

Digital Currency Ecosystem Resilience: The ability of the digital currency ecosystem to withstand and recover from shocks and disruptions. Resilience involves robust design, effective governance, and proactive risk management to ensure the stability and continuity of digital financial services.

Global Digital Financial Integration: The integration of digital financial systems and services across borders, facilitating international transactions and economic cooperation. Global digital financial integration aims to create a more connected and efficient global financial system.

Central Bank Digital Currency (CBDC) Implementation: The process of developing, testing, and deploying CBDCs. Implementation involves technical development, regulatory approval, stakeholder engagement, and public education to ensure the successful launch of digital currencies.

Digital Currency Ecosystem Scalability: The ability of digital currency systems to handle increasing transaction volumes and user demands. Ensuring scalability involves optimizing technology, infrastructure, and processes to support growth and maintain performance.

Digital Currency Ecosystem Collaboration: The cooperation among various stakeholders in the digital currency ecosystem to achieve common goals. Collaboration involves sharing knowledge, resources, and best practices to foster innovation and ensure the successful integration of digital currencies into the financial system.

Central Bank Digital Currency (CBDC) Pilot Programs: Experimental initiatives conducted by central banks to test the feasibility and implications of CBDCs. Pilot programs provide valuable insights and inform the development of policies and systems for the broader implementation of digital currencies.

Digital Currency Ecosystem Innovation: The development of new technologies, products, and services within the digital currency ecosystem. Innovation drives the evolution of digital finance, creating new opportunities and addressing emerging challenges.

Central Bank Digital Currency (CBDC) Security: The measures and protocols implemented to protect CBDCs from cyber threats, fraud, and other risks. Security is a critical aspect of CBDCs, ensuring the integrity and trustworthiness of digital currency systems.

Digital Currency Ecosystem Regulation: The rules and guidelines governing the issuance, distribution, and use of digital currencies. Effective regulation ensures the stability, security, and compliance of digital currencies with legal and ethical standards.

Made in the USA
Middletown, DE
24 July 2024

57687729R00156